Harry Edward Richards

The Mystery of Life

A Study of Revelation in the Light of Science

Harry Edward Richards

The Mystery of Life
A Study of Revelation in the Light of Science

ISBN/EAN: 9783337252953

Printed in Europe, USA, Canada, Australia, Japan

Cover: Foto ©Suzi / pixelio.de

More available books at **www.hansebooks.com**

The Mystery of Life

A STUDY OF REVELATION IN THE LIGHT
OF SCIENCE

BY

HARRY E. RICHARDS, A. M., M. D.

NEW YORK
DODD, MEAD AND COMPANY
1898

The Lord Baltimore Press
THE FRIEDENWALD COMPANY
BALTIMORE, MD., U. S. A.

CONTENTS

Chapter		Page
I.	Life,	10
II.	Kingdoms of Life,	22
III.	The Spiritual Kingdom,	39
IV.	Entering the Kingdom,	50
V.	Immortality,	60
VI.	The Sin against Life,	101
VII.	The Way of Life,	113
VIII.	God's Sovereignty and Man's Agency,	128
IX.	Cause,	144
X.	Free Will,	159
XI.	The Revelation of Life,	180
XII.	The Necessity of Faith,	214
XIII.	The Mystery of Revelation,	231
XIV.	The Reasonableness of the Revelation of Life,	267

INTRODUCTION

THE preservation and enjoyment of life constitute the sum-total of human activity. Upon analysis, every occupation of mankind and every device of the most complex civilization is found to be concerned directly with these things, and ultimately to have no other object. It is not a matter of surprise, therefore, to find that such matters as the origin, nature and duration of life are of universal and transcendent interest. Neither is it strange that religion, in spite of the scepticism of a few philosophers, should possess an irresistible attraction for most people, since it treats of a supernatural realm whose activities they believe directly affect the continuance and enjoyment of their own lives. It is also, for this reason, easy to understand why Christianity has steadily prevailed over all other religions; since, according to its Founder, it plainly declares its purpose to be that man may have life and have it more abundantly, and that, too, forever. The mere fact that it even makes such a claim is enough to command for it the serious attention of beings whose every possession depends upon the possession of life. Since, then, the one thing desired by each individual is life, and since the Christian revelation professes to point the way to the satisfaction of this desire, an investigation of the thing sought and offered becomes of the greatest importance, in order that it may be decided whether the offered means be even seemingly adequate to the attainment of the desired end.

In the argument concerning life which is to follow it is taken for granted that there is a God; that he is the Creator of the visible universe; that he has made a revelation to mankind as set forth in the Christian Scriptures. As a corollary to these postulates it follows that science, which is merely the systematized knowledge of the things created, cannot be in contradiction to the revelation of the Creator, and that if science and revelation seem to be in contradiction, it arises from the misinterpretation either of nature or of revelation, or both. It further follows, from the assumed identity of the Creator and the Revealer, that an apparent harmony of the teachings of science and the interpretation of the revelation goes to show that both the teaching and the interpretation are true. And finally, if it be found upon investigation that science and the Scriptures are harmonious in their teachings concerning the origin, nature and continuance of life, it will afford strong evidence of the truth of the postulates with which the argument is begun. This, however, is but an incidental result, since what follows is primarily addressed to those who are already convinced of the truth of these very postulates.

On account of the point of view from which the argument is made, it will be noted that nature and the Bible are both cited as authorities; there is no attempt made to prove the Scriptures from science, or to harmonize science and religion, but to study the Bible in the increased light of modern discovery. Science and religion are considered, not as antagonistic, but complementary.

CHAPTER I

LIFE

What is life? or rather how does it manifest itself? for it is much to be feared that life will never be satisfactorily defined. Indeed this may be said about all the forces of the universe. What they are will doubtless always remain among the inscrutable things of the infinite unknown. Man knows that light casts shadows, enables the eye to perceive objects, develops the green in plants, produces vigor in animals, affects the photographic plate, and travels through space; it takes no philosopher to say whether it is light or dark, but not even the greatest philosopher is able to say with certainty what light is. And so with heat, electricity and other forces of nature. Something is known of their effects, but little of them. They are all like the wind, of which we hear the sound, but whence it cometh or whither it goeth we know not. We know what forces do, but not what they are.

Life, like electricity, is detected by its manifestations, it is known by what it does. The best definition of life is probably that of Mr. Spencer, which is that "Life is the definite combination of heterogeneous changes, both simultaneous and successive, in correspondence with external co-existences and sequences," or "the continuous adjustment of internal relations to external relations." But after all, this is merely a beautiful and accurate definition of how life manifests itself; indeed, no more is claimed for it by its author. But inasmuch as all we know of anything is its characteristics, we know as much of life, in knowing how it manifests itself, as we know of anything. Life, then, in common language, may be defined as correspondence with environment. It manifests itself by the capacity of the organism in which it resides, of continuous self-adjustment to changing circumstances—by the organism responding to a change in its surroundings by a corresponding change in itself.

Since life depends upon the capability of the organism of making responsive changes to the changes occurring in its environment, life becomes more full and rich as the correspondence between the organism and the environment increases. The environment, for instance, of the oyster exhibits few changes, and the responsive changes in the oyster are likewise few and its grade of life is very low. The correspondence between the fish and its environment is greater, and all recognize in it a higher degree of life. And so the different creatures ascend the scale of life through the fishes, the reptiles, the mammals (the animal in the popular sense), to man, whose grade of life is recognized as the highest. In man we see exemplified the greatest number and variety of internal changes corresponding with external changes; the numerous complicated and varied changes of his environment are met in him by corresponding internal changes of equal number, complexity and variety. This principle, that life varies in proportion to the number and variety of correspondences between external and internal changes, is popularly recognized by the oft-repeated saying, that a man has been "existing" and not "living" while he has been compelled to remain in the midst of non-varying conditions. It is even more fully recognized in the common remark that certain people do not "live," they "vegetate"—vegetation being recognized as a low order of life. The philosopher, as well as the common people, presents the same idea, though clothed in other and perhaps more accurate language. Herbert Spencer says: "It is manifest *a priori*, that since changes in the physical state of the environment, as also those mechanical actions and those variations of available food which occur in it, are liable to stop the processes going on in the organism; and since the adaptive changes in the organism have the effect to directly or indirectly counterbalance these changes in the environment; it follows the life of the organism will be short or long, low or high, according to the extent to which changes in the environment are met by corresponding changes in the organism. Allowing the margin for perturbations, the life will continue only while the correspondence continues; the completeness of the life will be proportionate to the completeness of the correspondence; and the life will be perfect only when the correspondence is perfect."

This definition brings forward two principal ideas: the first, that the quality of life depends upon an ever-changing variety of circumstances surrounding the living being, coupled with the capacity of that living being to meet the changes going on about it with corresponding changes within itself: stagnation in one's surroundings brings stagnation to his life. The second idea presented is that death comes from a failure in the living being or organism to meet an external change by an internal change. For example, the frost brings to an end the life of the annual flowering plant because it makes no change within itself to meet the change in its surroundings. The water in its stem, which contributed to and rendered possible its life during the summer, freezes and destroys that life the first cold night of autumn. The elm, the oak and the other forest trees, on the contrary, with the approach of the cold send down the watery sap from twig and branch, thus making changes within themselves to counterbalance the change in their circumstances. Were it not for this, the life of the tree would be destroyed by the freezing of the excess of water within it. When the fish is left behind by the retiring tide and exposed to the air, it dies because it is unable to make a sufficient change within itself to meet the changes of its circumstances. A crab, on the contrary, is able to adjust itself to this same change of circumstances and continues to live. Animals from tropical climates almost invariably succumb when removed to northern latitudes, and many animals from temperate climates cannot live long in the tropics. Man, on the contrary, is able to meet almost all changes of climate which earth furnishes, and thus continues to live and thrive all over the earth. The average life is longer among the civilized than among the savage peoples, because civilized man has learned to accommodate himself to the changes in his environment. He has learned to protect himself from the dangers of heat and cold, dampness and darkness, and the thousand and one changes in his environment which would destroy his life unless met by corresponding changes in his own activities. Could man therefore continue forever to meet all the changes of his environment, with counterbalancing changes within himself, he would live forever.

It follows from these principles, that the greater the extent and variety of the environment with which an organism corresponds or is capable of corresponding, the greater the change necessary to destroy it. For example, young children yet unable to walk or talk, succumb to changes in their surroundings which to the full grown man would scarcely be thought worthy of notice, because in the one case the change relative to the power of correspondence is very great and in the other very small. It is because of their extensive environment and vast power of adaptation that of all creatures men are the hardest to kill. It might be thought that the horse, on account of its greater strength, would have greater power of endurance than man, but the fact is found to be the contrary. The change under adverse circumstances which both horse and man endure, in armies for example, may be exactly the same, but in proportion to the total amount of changes in their circumstances which each is able to meet by changes in his own conduct, the change is much greater for the horse than for the man. The result is death to the horse and continued life to the man. The same principle is illustrated in the case of people who have centered all their interest and affection in one person or one pursuit; if disaster overtakes this favorite person or pursuit they may and do die—of a broken heart, it is said. Really what happens is a change—a change so great in the environment that the person is unable to adapt himself to it, and dies. Had his interests and affections been more widely distributed, both as regards persons and pursuits, the blotting out of any one would have been so small a part of the whole that his power of adaptation, that is to say his hold on life, would not have been overwhelmed. Men of varied interests and attachments not only live a higher life but are likely to live a longer one.

Science has now for a long time indicated

that all forces are but different manifestations of one force; that all nature is but the varied manifestation of the Infinite Power behind nature. This one force, this Infinite Power, the Scriptures have always taught, is God. And if this be true, the one thing necessary for the eternal life of any living being is a sufficiently perfect obedience to God, that is to say, sufficiently perfect correspondence with all the infinite forces of the universe; because death comes always and invariably from failure to harmonize with some manifestation of the forces of the universe.

But to be able to act harmoniously with the forces of an environment demands a creature with attributes necessary to perceive the action of these forces and to accommodate itself to them. The fish is able to live in the water and the bird in the air because they are creatures whose very vital force produces in them capacities for corresponding with their environments. The human race exhibits creatures with higher powers of adapting themselves to the varied play of God's forces, or as they are more frequently called the forces of nature; but the various organs and functions of fish, bird and man are due to as many different kinds of vital force, which certainly and inexorably develop the creature in which they dwell each after its own kind. The most powerful microscope fails to show any essential difference in the eggs or ova in which originate the fish, snake, dog and man, but distinct and peculiar vital forces exist in them which will little by little differentiate the one from the other, and at length produce the very different creatures which they severally characterize. It is then the different kinds of vital force or life which produce the different kinds of living creatures with their varying powers of perception and action. From the standpoint of science, therefore, it would seem that if the problem of eternal life were to be solved, a new and different kind of life in a new creature was demanded, whose responsive powers would be great enough to meet the requirements, whose vital force would produce faculties sufficiently sensitive to perceive all changes in the environment, and powers sufficient to make the necessary correspondence; and this the New Testament declares to be the Christian doctrine. Let us examine this a little in detail.

That there are different kinds of life is a matter of the most common knowledge. Lowest in the scale, we all note the vegetable life, that which is possessed by the ferns, the grasses and the trees. While it is true that the very lowest kind of living vegetable organisms may not be distinguished by the inexperienced from the lowest kind of animal creatures; and while perhaps even the most experienced naturalists, when dealing with the very lowest forms of life, can scarcely tell the living plant from the living animal; still all mankind recognizes the fact that the life of the tree is not the life of the tiger, and that the life of the grass is not the life of the worm. Next higher in the scale, we observe animal life, and the world, learned and unlearned, notes that the animals possess a different life from that of the trees and grasses. The most of men may not be able to give scientific descriptions, but they know and realize that the animals are possessed of life peculiar to themselves, and the veriest savage would not hesitate to place the animals on a higher plane than the plants.

But now we approach a region of greater difficulty. That plant life and animal life are different things may be considered universally accepted by the acts and thoughts of mankind, but from here on the philosophers do not agree. One class holds that human life is more than and different from animal life, that human beings are not mere animals. Another class, with great force and vigor maintain that man is merely the highest order of animal. But leaving the philosophers for the time being, it is to be noted that the idea of the mass of the people, as evidenced by their conduct and by their language, is that man is more than animal, and that human life is a distinct kind of life. The frequent use of the phrase "human life" by all orders of men, and the sacredness of it, show that mankind places animal life in one class and human life in another. The same idea is shown in the determined claim that man differs from the brute in possessing a soul, which is only another way of saying that man differs from the brute in possessing a different kind of life. In fact this idea has become so engrafted in human speech that the word soul is often used to designate human life: as for instance when, in case of shipwreck or other accident, the reports state a loss of so many souls, meaning thereby that so many human beings were drowned or otherwise killed.

In addition to the plant, the animal, and the human being, both the Scriptures, and human beings in their ordinary thinking and speaking, recognize still another living being—a spirit. But while recognizing in act and word the existence of several kinds of life and several kinds of living creatures, mankind, philosophers included, seem not too sure as to their own conclusions. Ghosts and spirits savor of the shadowy, whether they figure in tales or treatises; and man and the animals in these latter times seem to have run much together even in popular fancy. If there be indeed different kinds of life and different classes of living creatures; if the human being is not merely the highest order of animal; and if the spirit life is something separate and distinct from animal life or human life; and if the eternal life which has been the hope of mankind in all ages is not a mere continuation of animal or human life, certainly the distinctions between them should be made most plain, and confounding them the one with the other should be as diligently avoided as the confounding of mushrooms and toadstools, quinine and morphine. For a failure to distinguish between them may be as fatal in the one case as in the other, if there be indeed a spiritual life and it be worth the getting.

CHAPTER II

KINGDOMS OF LIFE

No more valuable method of clarifying ideas has ever been discovered than that of comparison. We learn to distinguish one thing from another only by comparing their respective characteristics. We get our most cleancut conception of a thing from a careful comparison of it with other similar but different things. This process enables the physician to come to a correct diagnosis of the disease and thereby apply the proper remedy; it is pursued by the lawyer and judge in applying the law; consciously or unconsciously, every thinker and skillful worker arrives at precision and efficiency by an exercise of the faculty of comparison. By this method naturalists have classified all things under the sun; by this method they have established species, classes and genera, and finally, as they designate them, kingdoms, the characteristics which serve as standards of comparison becoming more and more important as we ascend from species to kingdoms.

KINGDOMS OF LIFE

The differences which decide between members of kingdoms are fundamental. When therefore the naturalist speaks of the mineral kingdom, the vegetable kingdom and the animal kingdom, he speaks of classes of things separated by the broadest distinctions. It seems that the use of the word kingdom in this connection is a particularly happy one. A kingdom is that which is under the dominion or rule of a king, that which is subject, in other words, to the laws of a king, that which is subject to the same system of laws. Therefore a kingdom means something more than territory. In reality, by kingdom is meant those persons who are under or subject to a certain system of laws, wherever these persons may be found, whether within the so-called territory of the kingdom, on the high seas in the king's ships, marching in his armies in foreign lands, or dwelling peaceably abroad. It is the reign of law alone that gives existence to a kingdom; subjection to its laws, and not mountains, rivers or surveyor's lines mark the boundaries of the kingdom. The individual subjects of the king are, as a rule, dissimilar in outward individual characteristics, but the essential qualification is whether they are subject to the laws of the king. Each kingdom has its own proper system of law, and all members of the kingdom conform thereto.

Obedience to a system of laws serves as the standard of classification, to distinguish physical as well as political kingdoms.

One of the great laws of the mineral kingdom or the inorganic or not-living kingdom is the law of gravitation; to this law all matter is obedient; the laws of crystallization and chemical affinity also hold sway here. So we find the unliving and inorganic matter moving upon the earth or held in its place upon it or revolving through space in obedience to the law of gravitation; we find the minerals and rocks crystallizing, and we find everywhere matter combined and combining in accordance with chemical affinities. But on the contrary we do not find any obedience to those laws which cause the watery sap to run up in a tree instead of down, or cause the plant to grow upward in apparent defiance of the law of gravitation; nor do we find any seed-time or harvest prevailing in the regions of the inorganic kingdom, or any obedience to the great law of the plant kingdom, the herb yielding seed and the fruit-tree yielding fruit after its kind. That which is of the inorganic kingdom is subject to the laws of that kingdom and to those alone.

But when we regard the vegetable kingdom we find a new system of laws, and we find the members of the kingdom uniformly obeying those laws. Each kind brings forth seed after its own kind and multiplies and increases; moisture and heat, which produce no such effect on the pebbles of the inorganic world, cause seed to sprout and the plants to grow. While the water in the brook by no chance ever runs uphill, in the vegetable kingdom we find the water from the earth taken up scores, perhaps hundreds of feet from the earth, in accordance with the law of the new kingdom. And as the time of frost approaches, when it would work irreparable damage to the tree, and yet before the frost is at hand, this same water is sent back from the twigs and branches into the earth. The only changes wrought in the inorganic world are the physical and chemical; but in the vegetable kingdom we find the atmosphere in passing through the leaves of a tree is robbed of its carbonic acid (a combination of carbon and oxygen), the carbon being retained by the tree and the oxygen sent back into the air; while the roots of the tree, on the other hand, take in the nitrogen and the potash dissolved in the water and these are converted into living matter under new combinations. Everywhere in every plant the matter of the inorganic world, the oxygen, the carbon, the hydrogen, the nitrogen, the potash are being wrought into living forms in obedience to the laws of the vegetable kingdom. A thing is a plant or not as it obeys or does not obey the peculiar laws of the plant kingdom.

As when passing the frontier of a political kingdom we become at once aware of different rules and regulations and laws of conduct, so when we pass from the plant to the animal kingdom we are soon made aware of the sway of an entirely new system of law. A plant in breathing takes in the carbonic acid of the atmosphere, breaks it up within itself into carbon and oxygen, retains the carbon and sends forth the oxygen. The animal, on the contrary, in breathing takes in the oxygen which unites with the carbon within and is sent forth into the atmosphere as carbonic acid, the animal and the plant thus playing complementary parts in their effects upon the atmosphere, the one rejecting what is needed for the other. No plant, be it moss or grass or fern or tree, can exist in an atmosphere without carbonic acid; no animal, on the contrary, could exist in an atmosphere without oxygen. The plant feeds upon the inorganic materials carbon, nitrogen, potash, lime and the like existing in the air and soil; the animal, on the contrary, cannot live upon inorganic material; its food must have passed through the laboratory of vegetable life. The food of the plant needs no digestion to fit it for assimilation, but the food of the animal is incapable of sustaining its life in the condition in which it comes to it. It must be digested. Hence the broad and distinctive characteristic of the animal is its stomach. Even the formless jelly-like amoeba seems to create or improvise a stomach, out of its homogeneous mass, as soon as a particle of food comes in contact with it; or, if one desires to so regard it, the whole animal is a stomach. The animal is thus again subject to a system of laws which does not prevail in the vegetable kingdom. The animal responds to and obeys the laws regulating its breathing and eating and other actions which have no application at all in the kingdom of plants. The animal is separated from the mineral kingdom by virtue of its being alive, from the plant kingdom by virtue of its being endowed with an entirely different kind of life, but in each case it is separated by being subject to a different system of laws—laws which the mineral and the plant are not subject to and cannot obey, because they are not animals, and which the animal must obey at the peril of its life because it is one.

The inquiry now naturally arises whether man is a member of the animal kingdom, or whether he is distinguished by peculiarities so fundamental as to place him outside of it. Is there, in a word, a human kingdom as distinct from the animal as the animal is from the vegetable?

That man's body is a development of the animal body might as well be admitted as now most probable. The records which geology has unearthed, of the life of the past ages of the earth, and the study of comparative anatomy tend to show its evolution from the most rudimentary forms of the digestive, respiratory, circulatory and nervous systems which mankind enjoys in common with all higher animals. Nor can man claim a very exclusive property in the formation of his limbs, which seem most to distinguish him from the other animals. Not a few species of animals use their hind and fore legs and their hind and fore paws in a manner very similar to the way in which man uses his legs and arms and feet and hands. The bear does fairly well walking upon his hind legs; the squirrel uses his fore paws in a manner not unlike mankind; so with many other animals;

and when it comes to the monkey the difference is small; and when at last we reach the anthropoid ape, anatomically there is as much difference between him and his next lower animal relative as there is between man and himself. So that if the elevation of man to a higher and separate kingdom depended upon the form of his body, or upon the operations going on within him of breathing and digestion and circulation and capability of varied motions, the case would be lost. It seems useless for the defenders of religion to any longer maintain a desultory and seemingly hopeless conflict where the battle appears irretrievably lost. There never was any need of the battle, to begin with, and much less is there any necessity for continuing it. The close relationship of man to the animal must be accepted as a fact, explain it as we may.

Man we may therefore unhesitatingly say is the highest evolutionary development of the animal kingdom. But is he not more? If it may be admitted that man is an animal, and also maintained that he is something more than, and therefore different from an animal, there is relief at once from many of the difficulties of the old theologians. They felt— and they were right—that it was impossible to harmonize the statement, that man was an animal, with the Scriptures; but on the contrary they could not answer the objections of geology and comparative anatomy, upon the theory that man was an unrelated being, specially created six thousand years since. The evidence of his descent from lowest animal forms, and the evidence of his inhabiting the earth for very much more than six thousand years, were fatal to the special creation theory.

The defenders of the Bible and of the Church seem in all ages to have been fond of encountering unnecessary obstacles. The book of Genesis does indeed say that God created man, but it says more than this. It says, "And God said, Let us make man in our image, after our likeness; and let them have dominion over the fish of the sea, and over the fowl of the air, and over the cattle, and over all the earth, and over every creeping thing that creepeth upon the earth. So God created man in his own image, in the image of God created he him." Now it would seem to the ordinary reader, without scientific or theological preconceptions, that man was already upon the earth; that is, the animal man, or the animal having the form of a man, when God said "Let us make 'man' in *our* image, after *our* likeness"; and that that which required the making and the creation was not a body, but a human soul with human intelligence. It is not to be supposed that the most violent stickler for the literal in Biblical interpretation would contend that man's body is the likeness of God. In fact, such interpretation would savor much of the sacrilegious. The likeness of man to God and the reason why he is the image of God consists in his possessing in some slight degree the foreordaining and other powers of God. This not only seems reasonable on general principles, but seems to be plainly indicated in what immediately follows after the announced determination to "make man in our image, after our likeness." Nothing is said, after the announcement, about man's bodily form, or his arms or legs or anything whatsoever pertaining to his physical characteristics. What follows has relation to something entirely different, viz., *dominion*, and that, too, not a small or limited dominion, but a wide and sweeping dominion; such a dominion as would be an utter impossibility were man a mere animal. The apes and the monkeys do not to this day rank as a conquering race; they stand no chance as against the elephants, the lions and the tigers, or even the dogs. But here in animal man was a form peculiarly suited to the purpose as the instrument of intelligence and reason, of which dominion is an essential and distinguishing characteristic. The earth and all it contained were devoted to the exercising and development of the newly created faculties of man, for "God said unto them, Be fruitful, and multiply, and replenish the earth, and subdue it; and have dominion over the fish of the sea, and over the fowl of the air, and over every living thing that moveth upon the earth."

Here is not only counsel which God held with himself, that man was to be created in his own image, but such a designation of his future activities as at once and forever distinguished him from the "brute creation." For what was the necessary creation for the accomplishment of this subduing the earth and having dominion over all the life of it? Not the creation certainly of man's body or of the animal man, because with the result before us we see that animals much stronger and very similar have made no progress in this direction. What was needed was something more than a living body however perfect. That something was that which we call the human soul; and that was what God created. For the record further says "And the Lord God formed man of the dust of the ground, and breathed into his nostrils the breath of life; and man became a living soul." It is physiological man, as we know, that is formed of the "dust of the ground"; and when God breathed into him "the breath of life," what kind of life could it have been but a life in the likeness of his own—spiritual life; and when as a result of the life-giving process "man became a living soul," the "living soul" or life, as the words are elsewhere rendered, was a new kind of life, different from that of the animal creation, and after the likeness of that of its Creator. It is the soul of man, with its power to reason, and its kinship to God, that has enabled him to subdue the earth, to obtain dominion and to keep it. Therefore when God created man in his own image, an entirely permissible construction of the passage in Genesis is that man existed at that time, as an animal struggling with animals on the earth, as an animal formed long since of the dust of the ground; that God breathed into him the breath of a new kind of life; and that in addition to what he had been before he now became a new living soul akin to God. The creation of the *human* man was the creation of his *human* soul or life; and therefore there arose a new and higher kingdom—

the *human* kingdom—whose members perceive and obey laws peculiar to themselves.

It may be objected to the view just presented that we ought in that case still to be able to find the animal man upon the earth. But it may be replied that, according to Mr. Darwin and the best authorities on evolution, a species better fitted to thrive in its environment than another closely allied species, always tends to exterminate the less fit species. If this be true—and it is scarcely to be disputed—then upon the creation of animals into human souls these newly created human beings would, according to the doctrine of evolution, be fruitful and multiply and replenish or fill the earth and subdue it, and in the process exterminate the less fitted and most nearly related species. Or it might be replied that if a species of animal like the anthropoid ape was selected, what believer in evolution could for a moment doubt that such an animal form, endowed with human intelligence, and becoming the source of a new species, would rapidly develop away from the parent and nearly related species and become as different from the anthropoid ape as mankind has since become. That a new race was provided for when God created man is further indicated by the statement in Genesis, "So

God created man in his own image, in the image of God created he him; male and female created he them. And God blessed them, and God said unto them, Be fruitful, and multiply, and replenish the earth." Because if the animal form existed on the earth at the time spoken of in Genesis, and God breathed into this animal man's nostrils the breath of life, and man became a living soul (in other words, became a human being), and God created the human being male and female, the laws of evolution would determine all the rest, and we should find mankind developing from the original species, and thus Genesis and geology would both be satisfied; thus the Scriptures, science and common sense be all of one accord.

While some naturalists contend that all life which we see upon the earth at the present day has been evolved from one original species of life, and even that this original life was evolved from inorganic matter, others, and those some of the most eminent, are content to claim that science only surely indicates that the present forms of living creatures have been evolved from a few original parent forms of life; and so far from contending that living creatures developed from inorganic matter in the first instance without special creation, they admit that there seems to be a chasm between the living and the not-living which the ordinary laws of evolution in nowise bridge over. It is to be noticed that Mr. Darwin frankly admits the difficulty of connecting, by evolutionary laws, man as we find him and the highest of the lower animals. He says: " No doubt the difference in this respect [mental power] is enormous, even if we compare the mind of one of the lowest savages who has no words to express any number higher than four, and who uses hardly any abstract terms for common objects or for the affections, with that of the most highly organized ape. The difference would no doubt still remain immense even if one of the higher apes had been improved or civilized as much as the dog has been in comparison with its parent form, the wolf or jackal." Mr. Wallace, Mr. Darwin's co-discoverer of the theory of natural selection, goes further when he says, " Natural selection could only have endowed the savage with a brain little superior to that of an ape." It is just here that Revelation supplies a leaf missing in the book of Nature. The doctrines of evolution, natural selection, the struggle for life, and the survival of the fittest, deduced from the records of nature, seem to admirably account for the descent of man from the lowest animals of creation, provided we contemplate man as an animal only. And in endeavoring to defeat the tracing back of man's descent from animal ancestors the theologians have been hopelessly worsted, because they have accepted battle on the chosen position of the naturalist—man's bodily organization. But the naturalists themselves indicate in their writings that they are far from feeling themselves on certain ground by admitting the " enormous " differences between man and the highest of the lower animals. They strengthen our opinion of their own inward dissatisfaction when we compare the almost mathematical precision of their demonstrations, so long as they are confined to anatomical and physiological departments, and their vague conjectures when attempting to trace man—the whole man, body and soul—from the animal kingdom. It is just here then that the Bible offers its explanation. Physical man existed when God took counsel as related in the first chapter of Genesis. Evolution had brought forth the highest possible form of animal life. Animal, man was, and animal he would have remained. Natural selection had produced its highest type. When God into this animal breathed the breath of his own life, a new kingdom appeared upon the earth, and man the animal became a *human* living soul, a *human* being. Upon this human being the inexorable laws of natural selection at once began to operate, and the struggle for life has developed man into what we find him to-day. Thus we are led to answer in the negative the question whether man may be placed in the animal kingdom, and to decide that in addition to the three lower kingdoms—mineral, vegetable and animal—there is a fourth, the human kingdom.

CHAPTER III

THE SPIRITUAL KINGDOM

HUMAN life is certainly a high order of life, but does it furnish the hope to its possessors that it is an eternal life? If we depend upon natural science, the utmost to be obtained is that such a thing is a possibility, and an indication in what direction to look for it. Apologists for the Christian religion have attempted to give the needful encouragement by putting forth the old heathen doctrine of the immortality of the human soul; that is to say, the doctrine which teaches that the life which human beings enjoy is in and of itself eternal. But the arguments from nature upon which this theory rests are most unsatisfactory. He who would believe in the eternal life must found his belief in the information furnished by Revelation, by the Bible; but the Bible does not seem to teach that the human soul is immortal *per se*. It does teach, on the contrary, that man is mortal; and in this respect it does not distinguish between his body and his soul. It also teaches that there is a kind of life distinct from the life of the human soul, and that there is a higher kingdom than the human kingdom—the spiritual kingdom, and that the life of the members of this spiritual kingdom is an eternal life. It teaches, too, in the most unmistakable terms, that the living creatures of the spiritual kingdom are subject to an entirely novel and peculiar system of laws, which are inapplicable to, and unappreciated by all outside the realm. If any one will attentively read the New Testament for the purpose of noting whether there is or is not therein described a kind of life (a spiritual life) separate and distinct from the human life; and whether there is or is not therein described a kingdom separate and distinct from the animal and human kingdoms; and whether or no there is therein described a living creature, who is a member of a higher kingdom than the human kingdom, that is to say, subject to different laws from those governing the ordinary members of the human kingdom, he will certainly observe how seemingly the plainest language is used to emphasize the truth that there is a life, distinguished as spiritual, so fundamentally different from the human life that its possessor is a new creature who can gain existence only by birth. He will also note that man is, as regards this new kingdom, dead; that neither the man of flesh nor any part of him lives forever, and that if he is to obtain eternal life, he can obtain it, not by fortifying the present life, but by obtaining a new kind of life. This matter will be returned to later on. For the present the human kingdom and the spiritual kingdom are taken for granted, and taken as utterly separate and distinct kingdoms, whose members possess entirely distinct kinds of life and are in fact different beings.

It may be objected to this theory that it involves a dual existence, that it necessitates two beings living in one. It certainly is open to this objection, if indeed it be an objection. Let us examine it. From the Scriptural standpoint this need cause no difficulty, for the words body and soul and spirit as representing separate and distinct entities, are used over and over again; and St. Paul most plainly insists upon the fact that he was composed of two controlling, or as he puts it warring elements, the carnal, or as we might say the human element, and the spiritual element.

Nor is the objection any more valid from the standpoint of science. We find things may be subject to two or more sets of laws and belong to two or more kingdoms. The citizen of one country or kingdom sojourning in another kingdom is subject not only to the laws of his own sovereign but to the laws of the sovereign in whose land he dwells. There may arrive a time indeed when it is impossible for him to any longer obey the laws of both, in which case he must give up the one or the other and cease to belong, as it were, to both kingdoms. But under ordinary circumstances the sojourner finds no difficulty in living under two kingdoms. Citizens of one city have been expressly honored by being made citizens of one or more other cities, thereby placing themselves under two or more sets of laws. This is still better illustrated in the case of the citizens of the United States, who are, at the same time, citizens of some particular State. It has frequently seemed to those unacquainted with the American system as though it would lead to inextricable confusion, to be obliged to everywhere live subject to two entirely distinct sets of laws, subject to two entirely separate judicial systems and two executive governments; and yet the citizens of the United States are seldom conscious of their double citizenship. They are enabled to live their lives as subjects of two kingdoms, as it were, without difficulty.

So it may easily be that man may be at the same time a citizen of the human kingdom

THE SPIRITUAL KINGDOM 43

and a citizen of the spiritual kingdom; he need scarcely ever be conscious of this double allegiance. The two sets of laws may, on most occasions, govern him so harmoniously as not to excite consciousness of there being two sets of laws. But just as the individual with a double political allegiance may find the extraordinary circumstances of war compelling him to make his choice as to which kingdom shall receive his sole allegiance, so man may find himself in circumstances where his allegiance to the kingdom of heaven may demand his departure from the kingdom of man. He may voluntarily violate the laws of human life and lose it, but in doing so may fulfill that strange declaration of Christ that " whosoever shall lose his life shall save it, and whosoever shall save his life shall lose it." Here the two kinds of life are set over against each other; the plain teaching is that under certain circumstances disobedience to the laws of human life will be necessary to the salvation of the spiritual life, and the preservation of the human life render certain the loss of the spiritual.

So again the same thing may be subject to two sets of physical laws and so belong at the same time to two physical kingdoms. The lime and the potash and the other inorganic constituents of man's body do not cease to be subject to the laws which govern all inorganic matter because they have become subject to the laws of the animal life as living bone and blood and muscle. Man as composed of matter presses just as heavily against the surface of the earth whether dead or alive. If dead he is subject alone to the laws of gravity, chemical affinity and the other laws which reign over the material inorganic world; but when man is alive, while he does not cease to be subject to the laws of the mineral kingdom, he becomes also subject to the higher laws of animal life. If then man is a double compound being, that is to say, subject at the same time to two sets of laws, why may he not be subject to three or four sets of laws and be at once a triple or quadruple being? That his material substance renders him a member of the inorganic kingdom, dead or alive, is certain; but that his animal life has just as distinct an existence as his material substance is likewise certain, because the mineral substance changes momentarily, yet the man is the same man. While not so certain, most people will have no difficulty in assuring themselves that the popular idea of the mind being something distinct from the mere animal life is a true one. It may not be so easy to prove, but it certainly is very easy to feel, that the thing, whatever it is, which is able to contemplate and examine and reason about the body and the animal life, which feels and is even able to contemplate its own moods and feelings, and distinguish mental pain from physical pain, must be something, and a something distinct from those other things, bodily form and animal life, which it finds associated with itself. Whether we call it mind or soul or ego or what not is a matter of comparatively small consequence.

The fourth being of this composite creature man is even less easily distinguished; in fact, without Revelation having directed our attention to it we might have had some indistinct intimations of its existence, but that is all. Philosophers like Socrates seem to have been groping after the idea of it, and the poets seem to have had visions concerning it; but not until Christ and his apostles described it, and showed us how to distinguish it, did its existence become certain. Only when Christ " brought life and immortality to light " was man able clearly to distinguish the fourth element of his being. Nor need the scientific people be surprised at this. The atmosphere has been investigated by the philosophers since philosophers were, and previous to the year of our Lord one thousand eight hundred and ninety-four it is likely that nothing was considered much more certain than that chemists knew the constitution of the atmosphere, and that wherever else new elements might be searched for, little hope of finding a new one in the atmosphere was to be entertained. And yet, lo! in these latter days we are introduced to the new element *argon*, which has remained undefined in the air until these late times, although its presence has been physically felt by every human being since the race began.

As in the case of the mind, so with the spirit, it may not be seen or felt, nor can its existence as a separate thing be proved to the bodily senses, but like the mind it can be perceived by itself, and like the mind or soul it is capable of detecting and realizing the presence of its fellows. We have no reason to suppose that cats or apes are conscious of the existence of the soul of man, although they are without doubt conscious of the existence not only of his body but his bodily life; an animal not only recognizes man as a body, but readily distinguishes a live man from a dead one, and acts upon the perceived difference. But the human mind recognizes the existence of other human minds, though mayhap these other minds are far superior to it in the scale of power and intelligence. So the spirit of man recognizes its own existence, and recognizes with greater or lesser clearness the existence of the spiritual life, not only in other things like itself, but recognizes the existence and discerns certain of the attributes of God, the greatest in the spiritual world. Nor is it any argument against the existence of spiritual life that it is not discerned by the infidel, be he peasant or philosopher. The animal does not discern the existence of the human soul in man because it has none itself; no more is it possible for the spiritual life to be discerned by those who have it not. There have been not a few who have denied the existence of love, and who have been unable to discern it when present; nor could its existence be proved to one who had it not and was unwilling to believe, because every act of love might be attributed by a willful mind to some other motive. But to the one who feels love, the feeling of it is the highest possible proof of it; mathematics could not render it as certain. So there may be valid proof of the spiritual life producing the most absolute conviction to one capable of receiving it, while the very existence of the same proof is denied by others.

Life then is not a simple definite term, even when considered most literally. It signifies several distinct things—several kinds of life. This distinction is brought to our attention in a thousand ways in nature, and is even more enforced upon our attention in the Scriptures. The distinction which is manifested to us in nature shows the reality of the difference, and the stress laid upon it in the Scriptures enforces the danger of disregarding it. They have done an ill service to mankind who have, contrary to the light of nature and the law of language, rendered the difference indistinct by fanciful and figurative construction.

Only long-continued forced interpretations of the language of the New Testament could have succeeded in blunting our perceptions to the difference insisted upon between the human being and the spiritual being. Let the New Testament be carefully read with this distinction fairly before the mind and the result will be startling. It will be seen that only by the greatest forcing of the terms *life* and *eternal life* can they be made to mean as in ordinary religious parlance, *happiness* and *eternal happiness*. The teaching is that a new life is born within those who believe in Christ, existing for a time along with the human life, but continuing on after the death of the human being.

Taking it for granted that the argument thus far unfolded justifies the acceptance of the theory of a distinct spirit life as a permissible working hypothesis, the following chapters will be devoted to the application of it to problems which both religion and science continually and persistently press upon the attention of mankind. If it shall help in their solution its utility will be apparent.

CHAPTER IV

ENTERING THE KINGDOM

THE origin of the principle of life is wrapt in the inscrutable obscurity of eternity past. The doctrine of evolution, instead of clearing up the mystery of the origin of life, merely places the mystery further away. Once granting the existence of living creatures upon the earth, evolution affords a plausible explanation of their development both as regards variety and perfection within certain limits. But evolution does not give even a plausible explanation of the appearance of life upon the earth; it does not even serve to bridge the chasm between the different kinds of life which we find distinguishing the great kingdoms. Professor Huxley was not even satisfied that it gave a satisfactory explanation of the origin of species, although he accepted it as a good working hypothesis. But putting one side the consideration of the first beginnings of life, science most satisfactorily shows that as things are at present ordered there is no such thing as spontaneous genera-

ENTERING THE KINGDOM

tion. The not-living never becomes alive, without contact with previously existing life. It is a matter of common observation that all trees and plants come into existence from the living seeds of living trees and plants, that all animals come into existence as the result of the life of pre-existing animals. The believers in spontaneous generation were therefore driven to look, for proof of their theory, to the lowest forms of life. It was contended that the swarming life which soon comes into existence in infusions of vegetable matter was the result of spontaneous generation; that is to say, that the living creatures which developed in infusions come into existence without the instrumentality of pre-existing living organisms. Many carefully conducted experiments seemed to bear out this theory; and for years, spontaneous generation, or abiogenesis, held ground against the theory of biogenesis, which holds that all life comes from life, that every new living creature owes its life to a pre-existing living creature. But at the present day scarcely a well-informed person can be found believing in spontaneous generation. The modern experimenter, more careful than his predecessor, and with greater experience, has shown that no form of life, however low, is ever generated when all living organisms are rigidly excluded. Biogenesis is now the universally accepted doctrine. Every living creature of to-day owes its existence to some previously existing living creature, and that one to a preceding one, and so on back and back until all trace is lost in the obscurity of the past.

Therefore if the members of the spiritual kingdom are possessed of a new life, that is to say, a kind of life peculiar to itself, then no member of the animal or human kingdom can gain entrance into the spiritual kingdom by merely perfecting himself as an animal or a man, because it is one of the settled doctrines of science that no life comes into existence except from similar pre-existing life.

There are two essential elements in every living being—the material out of which the living being is built up, and the vital force which builds up the material into a living being. Every living thing, whether tree, animal or man, is momentarily bringing the vital force which animates it into contact with the not-living materials about it. As these not-living materials are touched by the vital force they become alive; but the non-living materials have absolutely no power to lift themselves into life. The life-giving impulse must come from the higher kingdom. There is an impassable gulf between the living and the not-living as regards the not-living.

It is to be noted that the material of every kingdom is dead as regards the next higher kingdom, inasmuch as it is without power to gain entrance into the higher kingdom; only when the higher life touches and quickens it is it made alive with the life of the higher creature. The plant by means of its vital force lays hold of the dead oxygen, hydrogen and carbon and they become alive as a part of the living plant. Thus the dead elements of the mineral kingdom become built into and form a part of the living plant. So again the animal, which is not able to live upon the inorganic elements which form the food of the plant, brings into contact with its own vital forces the complex materials furnished by the vegetable kingdom, and the vegetable matter of yesterday becomes a part of the animal of to-day. The vital force of the animal has raised the component parts of the plant into a still higher plane of life. In a similar way the human soul requires for support of its life the materials produced by the animal organism. To be sure, the animal is not confined to or dependent upon any one plant, while man's soul and body, as these words are commonly used, are so inextricably united as to form but one individual. But it would seem as though this union of the one member of the lower kingdom with the member of the higher kingdom depending upon it for means of existence, was merely a different manifestation of the same principle of existence. And it would seem but a still further manifestation of the same principle if it were shown that the new spiritual creature, the member of a yet higher kingdom, might be dependent for existence upon the organs and functions and products of the human being.

But in all cases the plant must needs come into existence from a pre-existing plant, the animal from the animal, and man from man; no member of one kingdom is created except by means of the communication of the life of the kingdom through a pre-existing member of it. In like manner the new spiritual creature could never come into existence except by virtue of the vital force of the living Spirit.

While speaking of the passage of the members of one kingdom into higher kingdoms, and the building up of the products of one kind of life into the living creatures possessing other kinds of life, little attention has been given to the creation of new individuals. The personal element has been almost entirely ignored. The moment we consider individuals we are brought in contact with a not greater but a different mystery of life. The individual of all the higher orders of beings must needs be born. Once in the world of the living, the vital force of the individual takes unto itself and makes alive the unliving material about it, and as constantly throws off from itself the erstwhile living to become once more dead. It is common knowledge that the elements of the body are continually changing. So that life has been communicated to new matter of the lower kingdoms from day to day, and thus in a sense new life has been propagated. But in order to pass on this current of life, flowing as it were in the individual, to a new individual, through whom in turn it shall flow to still another new individual, birth is necessary.

In the light of these very ordinary truths of nature how clear is the answer of Jesus to Nicodemus, "Verily, verily I say unto thee, except a man be born again [or as it is in the margin, from above] he cannot see the kingdom of God." This is merely stating the experience of mankind as regards the creation of new individuals — they must be born. Christ is not excluding any from his kingdom, he is merely indicating the mode of entering.

These further truths of biology Christ next enunciates to Nicodemus, in reply to the latter's objection, "How can a man be born when he is old? Can he enter a second time into his mother's womb and be born?" Jesus answered, "Verily, verily I say unto thee, except a man be born of water and the Spirit, he cannot enter into the kingdom of God. That which is born of the flesh is flesh; and that which is born of the Spirit is spirit." Here are set forth the fundamental truths that life comes only from the living; that the creature to whom life is communicated is like the living being communicating it, and that the life-giving impulse must come from above. The life-giving power of the Spirit of God touches man, and he in turn is born into the kingdom of God and becomes a living spirit. No amount of effort on the part of man can gain him entrance into the spiritual kingdom, without the life-giving touch of the Spirit. As well might the sand of the soil or the carbon of the air hope to become alive without contact with the living plant; as well the grass of the field expect to become animal without contact with the grazing cattle, as that man should expect to become spirit without the touch of the Holy Ghost.

The words of Christ to Nicodemus seem the

plainest of the plain. There is nothing to indicate the figurative or the allegorical. "That which is born of the flesh is flesh." How could the ordinary generation of individuals be more tersely and comprehensively put? Rabbi and peasant could understand these words. And the second statement is no less plain, "That which is born of the Spirit is spirit." Birth necessarily implies a new individual; not an old individual changed, be the change never so great, but a new being, a new person, a new creature. Christ said without qualification there must be a new birth, that the new birth was from above. The new creature which enters the kingdom of God is not, then, the old creature changed, but a being endowed with life by the Holy Spirit, who possesses a life which is not the life of mankind. This in the inimitable language of John is driven home with blows most direct: "That which is born of the flesh is flesh and that which is born of the Spirit is spirit."

But not that there are two parental beings involved in the birth of the spiritual man. So far as we are informed by the Scriptures— and we have no other source of information— all the members of the heavenly kingdom are created by the power of the Holy Spirit acting upon human beings; therefore the sons of

God, as they are designated, result from the union of the Holy Spirit with humanity.

The beings which God created in his own image would be, according to biological science, the only ones capable of having their lives united with the life of the Holy Spirit, to produce members of the spirit kingdom. It is well known that living creatures very unlike each other never mate and never propagate; therefore man, the only creature having likeness to God, is alone capable of being one of the parents of the sons of God. In this connection the saying of Christ must be recalled, that in the kingdom of heaven they neither marry nor are given in marriage. The generation of the life of the heavenly kingdom and the relationships of its members must not be supposed to correspond in all respects with what we see on the earth.

Biology teaches us that the new individual is not wholly like either of its parents, but partakes of the characteristics of both; we should expect therefore to find the new spiritual creature partaking both of its heavenly and its earthly parentage. This was true with regard to the only perfect member of the race that the world has ever seen; Christ the firstborn, the elder brother, was the Son of God and the Son of Man; he was both human and divine. The Christian knows that he is human, that he is the son of man, but he also believes the Scriptures that he is likewise the son of God, the younger brother of Christ and a joint heir with him.

One of the tests to determine whether any living creature belongs to a species or to a kingdom is that it possesses the faculties of the members of that species or of that kingdom. Christ not only says, in speaking of the kingdom of God, that a man must be born again to enter into the kingdom of God, but he also says that this is necessary in order to even see the kingdom of God. John also says, "Now are we the sons of God, and it doth not yet appear what we shall be, but we know that when he shall appear we shall be like him; for we shall *see* him as he is." Inasmuch as "no man hath *seen* God at any time," and since those who are born of the Spirit *see* the kingdom of heaven and *see* Christ, the new spiritual creature has faculties to discern his own species which place him in a different kingdom from the kingdom of man, the members of the former having powers which transcend those of the human being as much as his powers in turn transcend those of the brute creation.

CHAPTER V

IMMORTALITY

The characteristic of the new spiritual creature which most excites the attention of mankind is immortality. There is not a word in the Bible directly to the effect that men are immortal; the Scriptures may be searched in vain for one unequivocal statement that man is possessed of eternal life. Science is silent on the subject; it simply does not negative the possibility. The Bible, however, does state in the most unequivocal terms that "the soul that sinneth it shall die," and in a multitude of places, that the great overshadowing reward of the Christian is eternal life. It must certainly be admitted that if the Christian's inheritance is eternal life, there is a powerful implication that those who are not Christians will not inherit it.

It is undoubtedly true that the belief that men continue to live in a future state is well-nigh universal among mankind, and so far as we are able to learn always has been. This almost universal creed, of the immortality of the human soul, was very early adopted by the Christian Church, and for many hundreds of years passed almost unchallenged. From the Christian Church this creed passed to the Christian world, so that during the Middle Ages the immortality of the soul was almost as universally accepted among all the civilized nations as the existence of man himself. Able writers have drawn from this "intuitive belief" an argument in favor of the inherent immortality of the members of the human race. To many this "intuitive belief" of the human race is proof positive, not only of the existence of the soul as distinct from the body, but of its immortality. So great force has this argument of intuitive belief been supposed to have, that disbelievers in the immortality of the soul have with great labor sought to show that the belief in a future life does not exist among certain peoples. Whether this belief is indeed absolutely universal or not is still an unsettled question in the minds of some investigators. But belief in the existence of a fact does not insure the existence of that fact. The belief that the earth was flat did not make it so; that it was a universally accepted theory that the sun went around the earth had no influence upon the rotation of the heavenly bodies, in obedience to the law of gravity; the earth revolved around the sun and the moon around the earth regardless of the opinions of mankind on the subject. Belief has indeed a mighty efficiency in determining results depending upon human action, but not in determining the existence or non-existence of facts independent of human action. A man's belief in whether he is in a dying state or no may have a powerful influence on the determination whether or no that be his state, but his belief as to whether or no another man be dead or not can have no effect in determining whether that other man be at that moment dead or alive. It seems hard in the face of our universal experience to conceive how the mere belief of the human race can have aught to do in determining whether the human soul is mortal or immortal; there seems to be no certain connection between belief and the reality.

The Church has been a loser by just the amount of energy expended in the conflict over the inherent immortality of the soul. Not obeying the spirit of the instructions of Christ to render unto God the things that are God's and unto Caesar the things that are Caesar's, the leaders of the Church have sought not only to teach religion, which was their own proper function, but to teach science

IMMORTALITY

and philosophy, which belonged to others. It seems so great folly, and so great waste of strength and energy, for the Church during the centuries to maintain as a part of essential religious doctrine that which is purely a matter of science. What had the opinions of Copernicus, Galileo and scores of other scientific men to do with religion? and yet the Church has expended untold energies in fighting losing battles in the domains of mathematics, physics, geology, and other sciences physical and metaphysical. If a doctrine be indeed contrary to Scripture, let the Church fight against it, but one would think that the countless humiliating defeats of the past would render the defenders of the Church cautious in maintaining as essential elements of the Christian faith their mere inferences where the Scriptures are silent.

It may be asked in all seriousness, is not the position which theology takes on the inherent immortality of the soul another one of those positions within the domain of science which, after the expenditure of incalculable energy, must be given up in the end as lying without its jurisdiction? If the Scriptures teach that the human race is an immortal race, then the vast amount of time and thought and energy spent in maintaining the doctrine is well spent; but if it is a matter upon which the Scriptures are silent, or at most make statements from which only doubtful inferences may be drawn; and if the Christian is in nowise concerned whether the doctrine be proved or disproved, then the Church should refuse to any longer expend its energies in profitless combat. It should also abandon the conflict from other principles than those of religious economy; many an army has suffered defeat by the loss of a non-essential position, which might have been and ought to have been abandoned in advance. Defeat is contagious, and sometimes it matters not whether the contest was over a large matter or a small one. It discredits the Church to have its disciples maintain that it is contrary to the Scriptures to teach that the earth is round and then have actual experience show that the teaching is true. In the absence of express declarations or necessary inference from the Scriptures, the inherent immortality of the soul is a question for science, not for religion to decide. And let it be here noted that the question of the soul's temporary existence after the death of the body is entirely different from that of its immortality. It is the latter and not the former which is the subject of the present argument.

The Bible has little to say, if anything, of the immortality of the human soul, but it is full of express declarations that the *believer* shall inherit eternal life. Therefore the Church is interested in defending the doctrine of the immortality of the Christian, and may well leave the fate of the unbeliever in the awful obscurity where it is left by the Word of God. Christ brought life and immortality to light, and pointed the way to them. Surely if life and immortality on the one side and their negation on the other be not incentive enough, it may again be asserted that though one rose from the dead and detailed all the mysteries of the hereafter, men would not be persuaded. Before Christ appeared upon the earth, man's future state was an unsolved mystery; beyond death all was gloom and obscurity, and the gloom and obscurity was full of unnamed terror. When Christ came, he stated in the most unequivocal words that the cause of his coming to earth was that those who should believe in him might have eternal life—immortality. If the race at large enjoyed this inestimable boon, how purposeless, according to his own words, must Christ's coming have been! But on the contrary, if the human being, although enjoying a very high kind of life, was not endowed with that kind of life which would be eternal; and if in order to secure eternal life it was necessary to be born into a new kingdom, and become a new creature, endowed with a new life, of which immortality was a distinguishing characteristic; and if the way to it could only be brought to light by God himself manifest in the flesh, then the coming of Christ was full of purpose.

The doctrine of the inherent immortality of the human soul inherited from the heathen world, once adopted by the Church, led to the necessity of interpreting the words "life" and "death" all through the New Testament figuratively, although an inspection of the Scriptures themselves gives no warrant for such construction. What could be plainer, to the ordinary reader, than the words of Christ above quoted if left to his own understanding? What person of intelligence, unwarped by theological teaching, would ever dream of here interpreting "eternal life" as "eternal happiness," or of interpreting the word "perish" by the words "be miserable"? Let us paraphrase St. John to accord with the interpretation given to it of necessity, if this figurative interpretation be adopted: "For God so loved the world that he gave his only begotten son, that whosoever believeth on him should not be miserable forever but should have eternal happiness." Those who would so turn words from their ordinary meaning should have good warrant, particularly when it concerns a matter of life and death. Nowhere does one find the word "perish" to mean "be miserable," or the word "life" to mean "happiness," when there is not a word in the context to give the slightest indication that the words are to be taken in any but their ordinary sense.

The great purpose of Christ's coming, therefore, according to his own declaration, was to bring life and immortality to light; the one great object he set before the human race was eternal life. The reason of this was set forth by Christ himself when he said, "What shall it profit a man if he shall gain the whole world and lose his own soul?" and again, "What will a man not give for his life?" Nor is it strange to the thinking mind that Christ should have held up life as the one thing necessary, because of what interest are the glories of heaven, or the happiness of those who pass eternity in the presence of God, to those who will not be alive to perceive and enjoy them? With life a being may be miserable, but he certainly cannot enjoy happiness without it; therefore the loss of life means the loss of all else. To place before the sentient being the glorious happiness of eternity, together with the knowledge that he cannot live to enjoy it, is hell indeed, as the word hell is commonly understood. To bring home to the intelligence of a man the fact that there is a future state in which beings who enter it will enjoy such "happiness as the eye of man hath not seen or his ear heard or has entered the mind of man to conceive," and then to bring home likewise the realization that this life, although once within reach, is not for him, because his life will soon become extinct, is to provide the materials for a regret and anguish not to be expressed in words. If these two realizations, that of the possibilities of eternal life and the certainty of death, are to be the fate of those who are not saved, little wonder that they will call upon the rocks to fall upon them, and that there "will be weeping and wailing and gnashing of teeth." The prospect of the loss of life under such circumstances would be a grief not to be borne. It seems logical enough, too, if one would sacrifice everything for a life of three-score years and ten, he should consider the loss of an eternity of life as a punishment great beyond the possibility of even feeling, with his present human faculties, to say nothing of describing it. To bring to light eternal life and to point the way to it to the human race seems a mission not unworthy of even the Son of God.

All must agree that eternal life is the all-important, all-absorbing reward held out by Christianity to its disciples. No one can read the New Testament and dispute it. To sustain its position, therefore, Christianity must prove that its adherents have immortal life, because if this be not the truth, all its other rewards sink into contemptible insignificance, and then Christians become indeed "of all men most miserable."

The possession of immortality by believers may be proved in one of two ways: first, by proving that the human soul is immortal *per se*, or secondly, by proving that while the soul may be mortal, immortality is conferred by God on believers. The proof of the first position, that the soul of the human being is immortal *per se*, at once does away with the great reward promised by Christianity—eternal life, so its adherents add the qualification that to the unbeliever eternal life is eternal misery, and that the real reward of the Christian is not eternal life, but an eternal happy life. Regarding the second position, that human beings are mortal, but that God confers immortality upon the believer, two views may be taken; first, that the immortality consists of the eternal prolongation of the present life, which is not here contended for; or secondly, that the immortality consists in the endowing of the human being with a new kind of life having the characteristic of immortality. The first doctrine, which might be called the present theological one, may be thus briefly stated: the human soul is immortal *per se*, and is destined to life forever in unspeakable happiness or unspeakable misery, according as it has believed in Christ or not. The second doctrine is that the human soul is mortal, but that there is a new life, characterized by immortality, obtained only through faith in Christ.

The holders of the theological view are driven to the maintenance of the inherent immortality of the soul, because their whole theory of Christianity must stand or fall with it; they have no alternative. Since the experience derived from the contemplation of things natural affords so little light upon the state of the soul after death, and since the appearance of things strongly indicates that death ends the existence of all terrestrial creatures, the believer in the theological doctrine turns naturally for the proof of it to the Bible. Here, since man's survival after death is so much against appearances, we should expect a doctrine of this importance, if it be true, to be stated with the most unequivocal distinctness. But we are disappointed; there is no such distinct statement certainly in the Old Testament.

To those who are thoroughly imbued with the teachings of the New Testament and with the thoughts and aspirations of the modern world, it seems more than passing strange that through all the centuries of God's revelations to the Old Testament peoples he never set forth the future life as the reward of faith and obedience. To Abraham and Isaac and Jacob his promise was not immortality for themselves, but his presence with them during their earthly lives, and a multitude of descendants, who should inherit the land of their sojourn and through whom the nations of the earth should be blest. To the nation of the children of Israel the promise was of peace and prosperity to themselves and their descendants, in the earthly land of promise. The prophets preached the blessings of obedience and the calamities of rebellion, but both the peace and the calamity were of this world and not of the next. Even when Christ appeared upon the earth he found the people expecting a Messiah who would bring them power and prosperity as a nation upon the earth. Not that the Old Testament has not many a glimmer of light which dimly reveals a future state, but the light is fitful and the glimpses but momentary. The burden of the Old Testament is the reward of the righteous and the punishment of the wicked, in this present world. Obedience to God meant flocks and herds, peace at home and power abroad; and disobedience meant famine and plague, invasion and captivity. One may read whole chapters and books of the Old Testament without even an allusion which would lead him to suppose that man was interested in anything except this present life, its joys and sorrows, its rewards and punishments.

The children of Israel were not cultivated up to the New Testament standard; they were immature in their ideas. Like all uncultivated peoples, of that and all other ages, and like the ignorant even in civilized lands, the future was of almost infinitesimal consequence as compared with the present. The savage will gorge and waste and sleep in the day of plenty, though it means starvation later on. Provision for the future is a late development both of nations and of individuals; only when a certain stage of cultivation has been reached are people willing to suffer present pains for the sake of future enjoyments. Abraham, Isaac, Jacob and Moses were men of minds far above the ordinary level of humanity; but the Israelites led by Moses out of the land of Egypt were a race of ignorant slaves. Their ignorance and degradation were doubtless great almost beyond our power of comprehension. The spiritual religion of the New Testament would have been to such as pearls before swine; they could neither have comprehended it nor have been affected by it. Esau who sold his birthright, which was future, on account of an empty stomach, which was present, is a type of uncultured man. It took centuries of schooling, wherein the sword was the emblem of authority, to fit the chosen people for the coming of Christ. It is therefore not to be wondered at that we see but faint reference to the future life in the records of the Old Testament times. The most that can be said is, that it is plainly intimated that the servants of God have a life beyond the grave, and that it is a happy life; and as regards the rest of mankind, there is a possible intimation of a survival after death in an inferior state. But the whole matter of the future life is so faint and dim in the Old Testament that it may be said with almost literal exactness that Christ brought life and immortality to light.

But coming to the New Testament, we do not lack full and explicit statements. We are told as in the Old Testament that there are beings of a different order from the human race, possessing a different life; " Before Abraham was I am," said Christ; an angel gave God's commands to Joseph; beings from another world heralded the birth of Christ to the watching shepherds; Christ recognized a prince of devils; he declared that twelve legions of angels were at his command if he wished. But not only did he plainly set forth that there was another world, inhabited by different beings, but he told his disciples, in the plainest of terms, that it was within their power to obtain an entrance into that other world, and that the object of his coming to earth was that man should not perish but have eternal life. He used no ambiguous language about this, neither did he only speak in parables concerning it; but he spoke in plain set terms, and made the most explicit declarations that those who believed in him should live forever. If there were any words capable of being understood by those to whom they were addressed they were such plain everyday words as "life," "eternal" and "forever."

Nor are we left in doubt as to whether these plain declarations on the part of Christ were understood by those to whom they were addressed. When Christ asked if his disciples would also leave him, Peter made the pertinent reply, "To whom shall we go? thou hast the words of eternal life." Christ not only revealed the fact that there was an eternal life, but he offered that as a reward of the believer; it was the inducement to come to him. Christ taught that it was an object of such transcendent importance that all else was as nothing when compared with it; it was the hidden treasure, the pearl of great price, for which a man should be willing to give up all else. The disciples and their immediate followers took the same view; the things of this earth were to them things not to be considered in comparison with the great object of the attainment of immortality. The writings of the Apostles glow with this same thought; poverty, hunger, thirst, fatigue, imprisonment and death on the one side, ease and comfort and bodily enjoyment on the other were veriest trifles less than air to these men, while they sought to carry the news of this wonderful possibility to their fellow-mortals. While the news that eternal life was to be had for the asking needed messengers, how could these men attend to ordinary things?

But note that while this great treasure could be had for the asking, it could not be had without the asking. It did not belong to a man as of right; it was to be had only by the believers in Christ, therefore no pains were too great to bring the knowledge of Christ to the people. Immortality did not belong to mankind, but could be obtained. Those who did not believe were dead—were destined to destruction. The apostles and their followers, "knowing the terror of the Lord, persuaded men." Death lay before each man. Death was a terrible thing, and the apostles strove to persuade men to avoid it. Thus far is plain statement; there is such thing as eternal life, and believers in Christ may obtain it; those who do not believe in Christ are already doomed to destruction; without belief in Christ they will perish. But the plain statements are all on the face of them against universal immortality. There are indeed parables and dark sayings from which it may perhaps be inferred that human beings as a class survive death; the length of the survival is not given, and, as before intimated, a temporary existence after death does not in anywise conflict with the view of immortality here contended for. The believer in immortality has many explicit statements to confirm his theory, if he confines himself to expressions concerning the followers of Christ. With regard to the race at large, he must resort to inferences more or less strained, and must construe many most explicit passages concerning the "dying" and "perishing" and "destroying" of the unbelievers in a figurative sense. Therefore it may be stated that a searching of the Bible reveals no such plain statement concerning the immortality of the soul *per se* as should be expected from its importance if true; that there are passages from which this doctrine may be inferred if taken by themselves; and that it involves a figurative interpretation of many passages which if taken literally would be fatal to it.

But if all human beings live forever, then the reward of the Christian is not life at all, but something else. That something else the common view says is happiness. This requires a figurative but not impossible use of the word life; of course if it be taken for granted that the human soul is immortal, then according to well-known rules of construction it would be necessary to give to life not its ordinary and commonly received meaning, but one which will harmonize with the ideas in connection with which it is used. The same may be said of the words die, death, destroy, perish. If the soul be indeed immortal and cannot die and cannot be destroyed and cannot perish, then these words must be given a figurative sense which will not make nonsense in the connection in which they are used; and under such circumstances the figurative construction given to these words by orthodox commentators is not objectionable. And were it stated unequivocally in the Scriptures, or were it capable of being proved to us by science, that the human soul is inherently immortal, the doctrines evolved from this figurative construction would not only not be absurd, but would leave little to be desired. On the contrary, if the passages of the New Testament in which such words as "life," "eternal life," "death," "destroy" and "perish" as applied to the soul and the future life, be approached for the purpose of determining whether they, in and of themselves, teach the doctrine of the inherent immortality of the human soul, it must be admitted that upon the face of them they do not, and the burden of proof lies upon the propounders of this doctrine to show that the ordinary meaning of the words is not the meaning they were meant to bear.

But accepting the postulate that the human soul is immortal, and the necessary corollary from this, that the reward of the Christian or believer is eternal happiness, and the conclusion inexorably follows that the doom of the rest of the human race is eternal misery. Once accepting the premise, there seems to be no escape from the conclusions of Calvin and Edwards and their school, without violating the fundamental laws of logic and doing violence to all our usual modes of thinking. The Calvinists have enjoyed the great advantage over their opponents in the theological field, in having a system. They have not hesitated to accept in fullest measure the logical conclusions from their fundamental beliefs, and do not find themselves therefore under the necessity of reconciling unavoidable contradictions. Every part of the system harmonizes of necessity with every other part of the system. Calvinism is a scientifically wrought-out hypothesis; and in theological controversy it has enjoyed all the advantages which an army has when brought into contact with a mob. But the burden imposed by the doctrine of eternal punishment, however admirable it may appear in theory, has never been patiently borne by the Church as a matter of practice. The whole thing is so intolerably repugnant to the human race that all sorts of devices have been sought to escape from the logical conclusion. Purgatory is simply the crystallization of the revolt of human feeling against logic. It rests upon the slenderest of scriptural authority, and has absolutely nothing gathered from science or human experience to defend it. It is simply a way of escape demanded by human feelings against the inexorable demands of human reason. The repentance after death so tenaciously clung to by a certain school of Protestants, is simply the Romish Purgatory with vague outlines. And even the most orthodox Calvinist in theory has in most instances repudiated by his living the result of his thinking. No doctrine can ever be satisfactory to the human race which inexorably demands either the sacrifice of human reason or of human feeling; and so the struggle goes on.

If the doctrine of eternal suffering be true it must be accepted, however dreadful and abhorrent it may be. But it is certainly in harmony with the kindly teachings of Christianity to avoid this horrible belief if possible. It is a terrible thing to be obliged to believe that God has created countless millions of beings whose fate is to pass an eternity of agony, as a punishment for a sinning extend-

IMMORTALITY

ing over an infinitesimal period of time, and this, too, when the sinning in most cases results from mere ignorance. This terrible belief is so repugnant to the feelings of normal human beings, and in such direct and apparent irreconcilable contradiction to the Christian's idea of God, that it is a grievous burden to the believer, and in these days a terrible weapon in the hands of the infidel against Christianity. Is there no escape? Let us examine the theory of the new spirit life and see.

The same objection lies against the new-life theory of immortality as lies against the theory of the inherent immortality of the soul, when viewed from the standpoint of nature. Science has no proof either for or against the immortality of the soul, and but little, if any, for or against the existence of spirit beings who are endowed with immortality. But this silence of science on the question of a future life is of greater significance than might at first be imagined; for the difficulties in the way of Christianity would be immeasurably increased if the doctrines held by faith were in direct opposition to the teachings of science, since science is neither more nor less than the sum-total of our knowledge of the works of God, and since the words and works of the same being should be in harmony. If they appear to us not to be harmonious, it is a matter of certainty that we must have misunderstood the works or the words; and it may be difficult if not impossible for the time to decide on which side the misunderstanding lies. Since then science teaches nothing, or but little and that very vague, concerning the future life, we can sympathize with Peter when he exclaimed, "To whom shall we go? thou hast the words of eternal life." Nor is there now any other course open to us than the one then chosen by Peter. Difficulties there are in the way of the followers of Christ now, as there were in the way of Peter and the disciples, and like them they have no alternative if they would have even the possibility of life. There is at present no certain word concerning eternal life, nor any teachings concerning it outside the Scriptures; we must learn from them or abide in ignorance.

Though there is no science of spirits or of spirit life at present, it is not a matter of certainty that there never will be. The world is still young, and who shall say what discoveries may be made of evidence of spirit life, when the industry and genius shall be directed towards it which have in past times been directed towards the elements of the sciences we know now. Pneumatology is no wilder dream at the present than geology, biology and modern psychology would have been not so very long since. But without waiting for the teachings of a new science, it may be asserted that the doctrine of the spiritual life is more in accordance with the teachings of modern biological and psychological science than any other propounded theory of a future life. If there be spiritual beings who are so different from mortals as to be called in the Scriptures new creatures, then that they should be born as Christ told Nicodemus, and that their creation proceeds from the communication of the life of a pre-existing Spirit, is in exact accordance with the teachings of science; and Christ's declaration that those who are not born from above—born of the Spirit—cannot enter the kingdom of God is merely a statement of biological law. Exclusion from the kingdom of heaven, and from the joys of the immortality which belongs to the creatures of the kingdom, ceases to be punishment in the way that word is usually understood, and becomes the announcement of one of the laws of creation, for the guidance of those who are willing to be guided. It is no more harsh than would be the announcement that the silica and the lime and the iron shall not enter the plant kingdom unless brought in contact with the vital forces of that kingdom, or that the proteid compounds of the plant kingdom shall not enter the animal kingdom except through the life-giving power of animal vitality, nor than the physiological statement that no creature should enter the animal kingdom except by birth. The doctrine of spirit life is not what science teaches indeed, but it is what the teachings of science might lead us to look for, and this is much more than can be said concerning the doctrine of the immortality of the soul *per se*.

But turning now once more to the Bible, and first to the Old Testament. The attentive reader of the Old Testament scriptures finds indeed little declaration concerning a future life, and, as before stated, the future life is nowhere offered as a reward to the faithful. But he finds a shadowy background of allusion to a world and a life beyond the grave. It seems that a future life is everywhere taken for granted. If it had been universally accepted by the people of Israel during all the period covered by the composition of the Old Testament that there was a life beyond the grave, the whole tone of the Old

Testament would be what we might expect. A matter that was absolutely undisputed and universally received and acted upon would need no declarations and would be only indirectly alluded to. And this is exactly what we find. So far from the silence of the Old Testament on the subject of a future life proving that the Israelites did not believe in it, there is evidence of considerable strength that the belief in a future life was no more open to question among the children of Israel than the rising and the setting of the sun or the regular succession of seed-time and harvest.

Seeking for a side light on this subject, it is a notable fact that the existence after death was a belief of nations contemporaneous with the children of Israel. The records of the Assyrians, Babylonians and Egyptians prove this beyond a shadow of a doubt. The Sadducees were in the days of Christ a school of then modern skeptics. They did not represent the ancient belief of the people of their own day. They were types of the skeptics concerning a future life in all ages; the mass of the people were not with them; the common belief of mankind, from now back to the dawn of history, and from the highly civilized to the lowest savage, is that human beings live on after death. But the trouble with this "intuitive belief" is, either that it proves nothing or it proves too much. Christ proceeded on the ground that it proved too much. "We are Abraham's children," and as such have inherited our present life and will keep it forever, was the contented sentiment of the body of the Jewish people; we were born immortal, and as Abraham's children will be the favored race in the next world as we have been in this. This comfortable belief of the ancient Jew has not been peculiar to him, it was shared by the nations about them and has been held by millions of human beings ever since. The Mohammedan is going to paradise, the Indian to the happy hunting grounds, the dwellers in Christian lands to heaven, and so on according to the varying creeds of the different types and nations of the earth. They almost all believe in a future state and that all will enjoy it.

So while Christ curtly and effectively silenced the Sadducees by the declaration that the God of Abraham, Isaac and Jacob was the God of the living and not of the dead, he found greater difficulty in overcoming the belief in the universal entrance into the kingdom of heaven. That Christ "brought life and immortality to light" could not mean that he first taught the doctrine of the immortality of the soul, because it is a matter of easy proof that this doctrine was the almost universal belief of mankind for ages before he appeared upon the earth. To give these words an effective meaning, or indeed any meaning, we must take him at his word when he said that the eternal life which well-nigh all his hearers believed in was not for all who heard him, but for those who believed in him and did the will of his father. It was not only to convince men that there was such a thing as eternal life that he came, but to overthrow the fatal error of believing that it was the common heritage of all mankind.

It was noted, in discussing what the New Testament taught regarding the inherent immortality of the human soul, that it would seem that a matter of such transcendent importance, if true, should be taught in unequivocal language and in plain terms; and it was noted also that this was not the case. Applying this same test to the doctrine of the spiritual life, it was found that Christ did declare in the most unequivocal terms that his kingdom was not of this world, not of this present order of things; and that the reward of believers was a reward mainly to be looked for in the new kingdom, which was not of this world. He taught that eternal life was the one transcendent object to be sought by mankind; he showed the immeasurable value of this object, when he stated that God himself had sent his only begotten Son into the world, that those who believed on him might have it. After setting forth this measure of the value of eternal life, language was powerless to describe it. May not this account for the fact that neither Christ nor his apostles make the slightest attempt to do so. Acting upon this idea of the value of eternal life, Christ taught that no pains were too great, no sacrifice, no not even the sacrifice of the present life, too costly to secure it. The apostles too were imbued with the same idea. And let it be remarked in passing that there is nothing in the language of Christ to denote that he meant anything different from that which his words signify, when used in their ordinary sense, as the people to whom he spoke used them.

Moreover, he from first to last taught that his mission was not one of condemnation, but of reward; he was the bearer of the gift of eternal life, not of death-warrants directed against the life that then was. "For God sent not the Son into the world to judge the world; but that the world should be saved through him. He that believeth on him is not judged; but he that believeth not hath been judged already, because he hath not believed on the name of the only begotten Son of God. And this is the judgment, that the light is come into the world, and men loved the darkness rather than the light." "He that believeth on the Son hath eternal life; but he that obeyeth not the Son shall not see life." The very plain signification of these words, and many others like them, is that the human world endowed with human life is, as regards the spiritual kingdom, dead; it is not dead as regards its own kingdom, but is dead as regards the kingdom above. Therefore it needs not that God visit it with any spiritual judgment, or if you choose, condemnation, because its own laws provide for its judgment; it contains the seeds of its own destruction. This is what man sees with regard to all vegetable and animal life; it has its birth, its growth, its decay, its death. Thus Christ stated with regard to the human kingdom what men knew to be the fact with regard to other kingdoms. The condemnation of those who did not believe in Christ, and by obedience to him put themselves in the way of entrance into the new kingdom, was the merely negative one of refusing the light and with it the life of the new kingdom.

Christ to show the way used the most common and homely illustrations, fitted to the understanding of the most humble of his hearers. They all knew what life meant, they all knew what eternal life meant. Nicodemus was not a biologist; but he need not have been, to understand that that life which could only come through a new birth was a different life from that which men already had, and that that which was born of the spirit of God must be different from the ordinary life of man. And so too the Scriptures state that the believer becomes a "new creature," in other words, a new creation, and that "that which is born of the spirit is spirit and that which is born of the flesh is flesh," and so on in many places. If these and similar words do not express the idea that eternal life is not for all men, that the only way to inherit eternal life is to become possessed of a new and different kind of life, and thereby become a new and different kind of creature, and belong to a new and different kind of kingdom; then supposing that Christ and his disciples had sought to teach such a doctrine as this, what language could they have used in order to make it plainer to mankind?

Not one of the least arguments in favor of the theory of the spiritual life is that it satisfies human feelings and does not demand the sacrifice of the laws of thought. No useless assault is made upon the impregnable logic of Calvinism. The desired result is accomplished by demolishing the postulate of Calvinism—the inherent immortality of the human soul. If it be discovered that the postulate of which Calvinism demands the acceptance is unreasonable or lacks sufficient evidence; or if it be discovered that there is another antagonistic postulate just as reasonable or for which there is just as great evidence, and that this other postulate if accepted leads to a conclusion which satisfies at once logic and feeling, then are we not justified in accepting, nay even enjoined to accept the latter theory? Now it is contended that there can be no argument drawn either from nature or from the Scriptures, in favor of the inherent immortality of the soul, that is not at the same time an argument in favor of the distinct spirit life; and it is further contended that there are many arguments in favor of the spirit life which are inapplicable to the theory of the inherent immortality of the soul; and it is further contended that the theory of the spirit life, if accepted, leads to such a harmonizing of thought and feeling, such a relief from irreconcilable conflict between the component parts of the human mind, that it should be accepted even though it lacks that certainty of proof prior to acceptance, which is just as desirable as it is unattainable.

No one finds fault with the appearance and the disappearance of the living organisms of the plant kingdom. The growth and development of a favorite tree is watched with interest and its death is a matter of sorrow and regret mayhap, but no one finds anything unjust or unnatural in either its birth or death. The same thing may be said about the members of the animal kingdom; from lowest to highest they come into existence in obedience to the great laws of the kingdom to which they belong, they live their lives in obedience to these same laws, fulfill the behests of the kingdom through their hunger and thirst, disease, sickness and death. While serving the needs of their kingdom, and still in obedience to its laws, they enjoy their lives; and it must be a shallow observer indeed who does not see that the overplus of enjoyment in the animal kingdom is very great, whether the animals observed be wild or tame. Had not the animal been called into being by the laws of life it would have had no enjoyment as a living being whatever; the pleasures between birth and death are the gifts of the kingdom in which it existed for a time. Having been called into existence, it enjoys life while it lasts; and when it ends has no fault to find, since what it has enjoyed has been, as it were, a gratuity. After it has ceased to exist it is as though it never had existed; and being dead, it is as though it had never lived.

And so we come to the human kingdom. If man be born into the world and lives his life in it, and enjoys the pleasures of it, and then departs from it, fulfilling the declaration of the law, "Dust thou art and to dust thou shalt return," where lies the ground for fault-finding? He has enjoyed the animal pleasures of movement and eating and drinking and sleeping, dwelling in the sunshine and communing with his fellows. In addition he has experienced the joys of humanity; the pleasures of mind have been his as well as the pleasures of body. "Man is born to trouble as sparks fly upward"; so with all the joys and pleasures of life there has been mingled a certain element of pain, which was not to be escaped; but in the human kingdom as in the animal kingdom, the pains in the life of the individual have subserved great purposes in the life of the race; and so comparatively insignificant in amount are these pains that only here and there one, and that one rarely sane, who does not tenaciously hold fast to life for the sake of its joys, forgetting its pains.

If then the human being is called into the human kingdom, and enjoys the life of it while it lasts, and at length, whatever that length may be, and whether the end of it be on this side of the grave or on the other, passes out of existence, he is simply conforming to one of the laws of life as he sees it exemplified around him on every hand. While in the land of the living, the relative proportion of happiness and misery which falls to his lot is regulated by his conformity with greater or less exactness to the laws of the kingdom in which he finds himself. Improvidence and intemperance tend to grief and misery, while prudence and temperance tend to peace and pleasantness. And while the results of these are masked and counteracted by the play of countless forces, so that their results are not always readily distinguishable; and while much good fortune comes to the evil and many a trial to the righteous, the overruling law undoubtedly is that virtue is rewarded and vice punished, and that man's happiness and misery depend largely upon himself. But over and beyond this (one might almost think for the purpose of closing the lips of the most wicked and the most unfortunate), the overplus of happiness in the life of human beings is so great that even the wicked enjoy life, the enjoyments of life being as varied as the living beings. So that if man is born into the realm of the living, enjoys the pleasures of the kingdom for a season, and then dies out of it, he is as though he had never been born into it. Certainly he would not contend that he had any pre-existing rights to be born into the kingdom. Then if the results of his creation are happy results, as far as they go, how does it lie in his mouth to find fault because they are not longer continued? "Shall the clay say unto the potter, what makest thou?"

If to fulfill the infinite designs of the universe, God has seen fit to raise the not-living into the kingdom of the living, and the existence of the living is on the whole a very happy existence; and then these same designs involve the passage of the living into the not-living again after a season of existence; if out of dust man is created, and after living his life, to dust he return, how can God be charged with injustice either on account of his birth or his death? It merely comes down to that which in ordinary affairs of life is regarded with repugnance, the demanding of the giver why he does not give more. Therefore when one contemplates the countless thousands of thousands of human beings who have come into and gone out of the world without knowledge of God, and to whom life and immortality were not brought to light, he should have no other or different feelings than he would have had God never created them at all. In that case they simply would not have lived, and as it is, they have or will simply cease living, and all things remain as they were.

So then, if the human being be a mortal being in the economy of the universe, and Christ's mission was to enforce upon the attention of the human race the reality and attainability of life eternal, full of a happiness incomprehensible, then God appears a God of love without need of explanation, then the destruction spoken of in the Scriptures is only that natural destruction which we must see is a part of the constitution of things, and which is dreadful only when needless. The punishment of unbelievers is thus only that natural punishment which follows from not taking possession of those things within our reach, and eternity will not be peopled with an infinitesimal minority of the happy and an infinite majority of the wretched, the former enjoying, or at least being undisturbed by the state of the latter.

The state of affairs exemplified by Jacob and Esau has always been a sore puzzle to the ordinary believer. Some theologians have indeed, seemingly to their own satisfaction, shown why it is proper that a mean-spirited believer should stand on a higher plane than the noble and generous infidel; but to the common people it is a matter of grave trouble. Does not the creation of a new creature, having a new kind of life, fitted to a different environment, solve this perplexing mystery? Who has not contemplated some magnificent dog or horse, full apparently of sensitiveness, generosity and self-sacrifice, to the disadvantage of some low-lived member of the human race? Who has not sometimes had a little sympathy with that distinguished writer who declared, the more she saw of men the better she liked dogs, when he has contemplated some more than ordinarily contemptible man or some more than ordinarily noble-looking dog? And yet with all this we never hesitate to put the life of the meanest human being on a higher plane than that of the noblest animal. We instinctively recognize the fact that we are comparing beings of different kinds, and that comparison is therefore, except in particular points, an impossibility. Certain traits of a noble dog compel us to place him far above some human beings, so long as we confine our attention only to the few points which in the dog so command our admiration. But upon closer inspection we discover that after all we admire the dog merely as a dog, and that we despise the man under comparison merely as a man. But when the dog, even the most noble one, is viewed as a whole with his capacities visible and latent, and compared with even the poorest specimen of the human race with his powers and capacities present and future, the dog cannot for an instant bear comparison. The difficulty experienced in the comparison of the noble specimens of unbelievers with the weaker specimens of Christians is, that we forget or are not aware of the fact that we are comparing members of different races. Contemplated merely as human beings, many a believer cannot stand comparison with many an unbeliever, just as many a human being regarded as a mere animal is completely outclassed by many a dog or horse. But if we realize that the believer has been born into a new kingdom; that the new spiritual creature is young and weak, is entirely overshadowed by the merely human and animal elements with which he is surrounded, but is nevertheless endowed with a capacity for growth and development which has an eternity before it; and if we also realize faintly what the end of that growth and development may be, we may understand why, in spite of the great superiority of the unbeliever in certain particulars, the Christian must be put on a higher plane by virtue of the new life within him. It is not merely what the Christian is, but what he has the power of becoming, that places him above the greatest of mere men. Is not this the explanation of Christ's statement concerning John the Baptist? Not among the children of men had a greater ever been born than John the Baptist, and yet the least in the kingdom of heaven was greater than he. John was a great man, he was great among the greatest indeed, judged merely by human standards. In vigor of frame and in power of intellect never had a greater appeared. Neither Alexander, Hannibal nor Caesar had surpassed him in native genius. But since considered as a child of the human kingdom he was but for a moment of time, the least child in the kingdom of heaven, with eternal life as his possession and its infinite possibilities as his inheritance, was his undoubted superior.

Thus it is seen that the theory of a spirit life which is a life distinct from human life, and which demands the creation of a new being, involves no absurdity, but on the contrary is what we from analogy should be led to look for. And further, this theory relieves us from many difficulties involved in other theories; in fact it enables us to harmonize the teachings of the Scriptures with both our experience, our methods of thought, and our inborn sensibilities. It further enables us to conceive of God as fore-ordaining and fore-knowing all things, which seems to be a necessity, without at the same time doing violence to our conception of God as a being of infinite love and infinite justice.

CHAPTER VI

THE SIN AGAINST LIFE

IN dwelling upon the beauties and mysteries of the Christian religion, in the enticing study of the character of Christ, the intensely practical quality of Christianity is in some danger of being lost sight of. After all, salvation is the great concern, and this is a matter, not of dreaming and musing, but of doing. The question of overshadowing importance which comes home to every human being is, supposing there be a future life, how is he to make sure of it. The preacher, from the time of the apostles even until now, has always found his initial labor to be the convincing of his hearers that they have any need to listen. Those who are well need no physician, and those who think they are well will have none; and convincing or, to use the technical word, conviction of sickness must inevitably precede the call for the remedy. It is a matter of the most common experience that it is sometimes more difficult to persuade some ailing man to "send for a doctor" than it is for the doctor to effect a cure when once called in. Most people will easily recall cases where life has been endangered and perhaps lost through failure of the patient to realize in time that there was anything the matter with him. How continually are parents and teachers obliged to labor with the younger members of the community to convince them that conduct which seems to them harmless enough is in reality full of danger.

The Scriptures and science both teach that the end of the human race is death, that there is no need of the issuing of any new edict, of pronouncing any new judgment; that measured by the yard-stick of time, to say nothing of eternity, every human being is as good as dead. What a common thing it is for one having received a mortal wound or being stricken with a fatal disease, to say, while yet living, "I am a dead man." And in the broadest sense we recognize that he speaks the literal truth. The fact that he has a few hours or a few days or a few months to live seems to him and to others a matter of such small consequence that no one ventures to gainsay him when he declares that he is dead. How apt, therefore, and how in consonance with our feelings and understanding, are the declarations of Christ and the apostles that the world is a "dead" world and that the human race is "dead"—dead because the span of life still remaining is too small to be considered in comparison with the eternity beyond. If a person believe either that his present life will go on forever, in any case, or that life for him ceases at the grave, in any case; or that supposing his present life goes on forever, his present conduct in nowise interferes with the enjoyment of his future life, he has no incentive to inquire what he must do to secure eternal life. Therefore it is that the preacher finds that a conviction of the falseness of his position, in the mind of his hearer, must precede all else. In the language of religion, man must first be "convicted," convinced of "*sin.*"

The inquiry now arises, what is sin? The laws enunciated in the Bible, the laws of the state and the laws of nature, show that sin is merely nonconformity to law—nonconformity to the law of the kingdom to which the being belongs. It was a sin worthy of death, under the reign of the old Hebrew law, to gather sticks on the Sabbath, but it was not a sin at all to the Egyptian, the Syrian or the Babylonian, let alone being a sin worthy of death. Under the Hebrew law gathering sticks on the Sabbath and murder were sins of the same grade, or at least were worthy of incurring the same punishment; but under the laws of Christianity and of the nations of to-day, murder is a sin of the highest grade, while gathering sticks on the Sabbath is no sin at all. Continuance under water is a sin on the part of a land animal, insuring the punishment of death, while on the part of the fish it is not only allowable but necessary conduct, because in the one case it is a violation of the laws of his kingdom, and in the other conformity thereto. Nor is the same conduct always sinful or always harmless to the members of the same kingdom. The taking of human life by human beings is sin or not according to whether it conforms to or violates the law of the state. The burglar who kills the householder is put to death, while the householder who in defence of life and property kills the burglar not only receives no punishment but is considered by society to have done a worthy act.

The laws of society recognize two kinds of crime or sin, *malum prohibitum* and *malum in se*. That is to say, first, those things which are wrong merely because they are prohibited by a positive law, for example driving on the wrong side of the street or upon the sidewalk, which acts in and of themselves have no element of wrongdoing in them; and second, those things which are wrong in themselves, such as murder, robbery, arson, which are regarded by the human conscience as wrong whether prohibited by any positive law or no. So that under human laws as well as under the laws of nature, sin may or may not carry with it any idea of what is known as moral wrong. According to varying circumstances, the same conduct may bring a man to execution as a traitor to his country, or elevate him to the throne as the savior of that same country. Therefore it does no violence to our ordinary conception of law and sin and punishment if we regard the whole human race as sinners, whose conduct insures death itself, and yet without any taint of moral wrong. The man who falls over the cliff into the deep sea has been guilty of no moral wrong, yet he sins against the laws of his kingdom to such an extent that his punishment is death itself. Had he murdered a man his fate would have been the same—death.

These considerations lead us to notice that there is a difference between *a* sin and sin. *A* sin is some separate and distinct and occasional violation of law. Sin, on the contrary, is a continuing, consistent and persistent course of sinning or violation of law.

Very good people from time to time violate some law of their kingdom or state and yet are not considered criminals, and so very good Christians from time to time violate some law of the kingdom of God and nevertheless they are not called sinners. The criminal, strictly speaking, is the habitual rebel against the laws of the state, and the sinner, strictly speaking, is the habitual rebel against the laws of the kingdom of God. So, too, habitual criminals are found to perform many virtuous and commendable actions, remaining nevertheless criminals in the general current of their lives; so that, notwithstanding many good and noble actions on their part, and the display perhaps of many of the most commendable traits of human nature, their state of rebellion towards the law renders them the enemies of society and demands their separation from it. The anarchist and the rebel against the constituted authority of the state may have personally all the moral virtues which ever adorned a human being, but the good of the state and the salvation of society demand their ruthless expulsion, notwithstanding the possession of such personal graces. Thus, too, so-called good people, endowed with every personal grace of human character, may nevertheless be the veriest

THE SIN AGAINST LIFE 107

sinners, since they will not acknowledge either the existence or the sovereignty of God and his kingdom.

The state would regard the violation of many of its positive laws by an enthusiastic patriot with the utmost leniency, while it would regard the determined defiance of its authority as a sin not to be tolerated on the part of one whose personal character was above reproach.

Then, too, the laws of different kingdoms do not always harmonize with each other. The very acme of goodness and sinlessness and obedience, as regards the laws of one kingdom, may involve the most unpardonable sin as regards the laws of another. The spy, who with the most sublime exhibition of self-sacrifice and patriotism goes within the lines of the enemy, finds himself there transformed into a criminal of the deepest dye. The hero on the one side of the line becomes the criminal on the other. Glory awaits him in the one kingdom and ignominy and death in the other; and all this, too, without any taint of moral wrong.

Leaving the kingdoms of society and entering the kingdoms of nature, we find the same laws holding good. We find occasionally, nay even frequently, violation of single ordinances of the kingdoms punished indeed, but pardoned after punishment; but a continuous refusal or neglect to submit to the law of the kingdom is fatal. The sand of the field may remain outside the realm where the laws of the plant life hold sway; that sand is thus, as it were, in a chronic and hopeless state of disobedience or non-obedience to the laws of the plant kingdom; it has no part nor lot in the life of the grass of the fields or the trees of the forest. And so again with the animal kingdom; that which lies without the sphere within which its laws prevail and its forces work is excluded from all participation in the privileges of the kingdom. There is naturally no idea of fault connected with the elements mineral or organic which do not come within the range of the vital force of the vegetable or animal kingdom, but the law remains, that not having become subject to the laws of the kingdom and the forces of it, they cannot become part of it.

In the case of life, the law of biogenesis holds sway at the threshold. This law is, as it were, the warder of the kingdom; through his gate all must pass which would enter; and pervading all of the kingdoms of life is the law that what does not enter shall partake of none of the privileges or activities of the kingdom; in the kingdoms of life we do not find anything corresponding to the non-residence of members of political kingdoms. Having entered a kingdom of life, many infractions of its laws may be tolerated, provided the violator accept the punishment annexed, and his sins may be said to be pardoned inasmuch as after the punishment he continues to enjoy the privileges of the kingdom. But there is one law which must be observed in the very beginning: failure to comply with it is not punished within the kingdom, but without it; its violation is an unpardonable and fatal offence. It is unpardonable because in the nature of things it cannot be pardoned: the punishment is concomitant with the sin and fatal to life and therefore there can be no pardon. This law which has these strange characteristics is once more the law of biogenesis, which ordains that what is without the kingdom must be brought in contact with the life-giving force of the kingdom in order to become alive and thus enter the kingdom. That which does not come in contact with the pre-existing life of the kingdom remains dead, remains in a state of continuing and universal disobedience or nonconformity to the whole system of laws of the kingdom; it neither perceives nor can perceive either the laws of the kingdom or the members of it; and by force of necessity cannot obey any of the laws of the kingdom and cannot exist within it: in fact it never enters the kingdom. Therefore a refusal or neglect on the part of those who are without a kingdom, to come within the range of the play of its forces, is as regards that kingdom an unpardonable sin. There is no use praying for forgiveness of such a nonconformity to law as this. It is a nonconformity to law which is inherently fatal to an entrance into the kingdom. This is sound science. It is also sound religion. If there be a kingdom of God, a spiritual kingdom, which is not the kingdom of this world, is not the human kingdom; and if it has a life peculiar to itself; and if, as in all other cases in all the kingdoms of life, there is no entrance into it except through the operation of the law of biogenesis, except through the bringing of that which is outside the kingdom into contact with the life-giving power of the kingdom, Christ could have used no more accurate words than those which he did use to characterize the one unpardonable sin. The unpardonable sin was, in his language, the sinning against the Holy Spirit; and that was a sin of such a nature that it was useless even to pray

THE SIN AGAINST LIFE

for its forgiveness. The sin against the Holy Spirit, as learned from other passages of Scripture, is simply a refusal to subject oneself to the life-giving power of the Spirit. Those who had received the principle of life from the life-giving contact with the Spirit might do many evil things; they might fail to conform to many of the laws of the kingdom into which they had gained entrance, and, while punished indeed, be nevertheless forgiven seventy times seven times. But those who refused to enter the kingdom at all, who remained out of contact with the life-giving Spirit, who were therefore not born into the kingdom at all, how could they be forgiven? It was inherently an unpardonable sin, that is to say, an unpardonable nonconformity to an universal law of life, a nonconformity such that it involved impossibility, not only of obeying the laws of the kingdom, but even of entering it, or worse still, even of seeing it. The unpardonable sin is no violation of any law of human morals, it is simply and solely the refusal or neglect to bring oneself or allow oneself to be brought within the range of the living force of the spiritual kingdom. It is unforgivable and unpardonable only so long as continued in. It is not something done once which no consequent conduct can undo, but a continuing course of conduct which cannot be forgiven so long as persisted in, but which involves forgiveness instantly and completely the moment it gives way to submission to the influence of the life-giving Spirit.

CHAPTER VII

THE WAY OF LIFE

CONVINCED of sin, convinced, that is to say, that his present actions and course of conduct are not in conformity with the laws of that kingdom in which alone life is eternal, one is prepared for "*conversion.*" And here again is found another technical religious word. Conversion is the logical sequence of conviction. A man when he is convinced that he is in the wrong way naturally turns to the right one.

Entrance into all other kingdoms of life except the spiritual kingdom depends entirely upon the forces emanating from within the kingdom. The minerals enter the plant kingdom through no exertion of their own; they are dependent upon the vital forces of the plant working upon them. They are powerless to in anywise further their own entrance into the kingdom; and so it is with the animal kingdom. The elements which come from without have no power themselves to do anything towards furthering their entrance into the kingdom. Nor is it possible for the living organisms of one kingdom to create for themselves an entrance into the next higher kingdom, either with or without the loss of individuality. Nor is it possible for the organisms of the higher kingdoms to open the gates of their kingdom to the organisms or individuals of a lower. There is an impassable gulf fixed between them, so that neither on the one side nor the other can anything be done to create a passage for individual organisms from the one into the other; what passage there is must always be at the expense of individuality; some of the constituent elements of the organism or individual make the passage, but never the organism itself.

There is only one exception to this wellnigh universal rule prevailing between the various kingdoms of life, and that exception is made in favor of man. To him alone is given the power not only to perceive that there may be another and a higher kingdom, but to himself fulfill the conditions necessary to enter it. On the other side the Spirit is always willing to open the gate into the higher kingdom; not only is the exception made on the human side, but also on the spiritual side. The life-giving power of the superior realm is able to open the way of entrance to the organisms of the lower, and effect what is so properly called in Scripture a *transformation*: a new creature is indeed created, but it is a creation by transformation; the individuality of the old is not lost in the creation of the new. Moreover, it is so ordained that man himself not only may, but must act in the matter; with the God-like characteristics of the human being come equivalent responsibilities. If he would pass from the human to the spiritual kingdom he must perform such acts as to place himself in such a condition that the power of the Spirit may take effect. The seed is the same in every case, but it depends upon the ground whether the seed springs up into life. The condition necessary to the taking effect of the spiritual forces depends upon the conduct of man himself; and therefore if ordinary conduct of mankind does not prepare for the reception of the life-giving power of the Spirit, man must actively "turn from the error of his ways"; he must turn from the old course of conduct to the required new one. And this is *conversion*. When, yielding to proper influence, one turns from the conduct which leads to destruction in the near future to that which constitutes the way to eternal life, he is properly said to have been "converted."

This conversion is just as necessary in the case of the good man as the bad, judged by human standards; because the most noble creatures of the human race, the strong, the beautiful, the generous, the noble and the loving among men and women, are subject to the laws of their kingdom, and the laws of that kingdom work out for best and worst one inevitable result, and that result is death. It is according to sound physiological as well as scriptural doctrine that "in the midst of life we are in death." Man begins to die as soon as he begins to live, and the same laws which carry on his life carry him just as steadily on to death. But because the idea of moral guilt has been so interwoven with the idea of sin, it is difficult for the good and the noble to comprehend that there is a disobedience to law, a sin which, without any moral taint, is unpardonable and not even to be prayed for. The very fact that the moral and the good break so few of the laws of the state, of society, of humanity, renders it hard for them to appreciate that they are nevertheless sinners, and are not only sinners, but are in a certain fatal state of sin which, as the universe is constituted, admits of no pardon or forgiveness. It is hard for such to realize that the publicans and the sinners, as they have viewed them, the breakers of human laws, harlots, thieves and murderers mayhap, may enter into the kingdom of heaven while they themselves may be excluded. To those who are so obedient to the laws of one kingdom it is exceedingly difficult to realize that they are fatally disobeying the fundamental laws of another. Is there not here an explanation of why Christ himself found his converts, that is to say those whom he was able to turn from their old conduct to the required new one, among the publicans and sinners, while the Pharisees, righteous according to their own law, turned to him a deaf ear? And is there not here an explanation of what every pastor in the land discovers for himself, that it is easier to gain converts in the streets and the alleys, among the lawbreakers and those who violate morals and sometimes even decency, than among the eminently respectable unbelievers who neither break the laws of the land nor those of morality.

Christ was not indulging in sarcasm when, commenting on the observance by the Pharisees of the rules of their order, he said, "Verily, verily I say unto you they have their reward"; he was speaking the sober truth. These men were moral men, sober in their lives; they obeyed the law of the state and performed all the ceremonies of their religion. They were the eminently respectable men of their day, and received the merited reward attached to obedience to law. As this world goes, their ways were to them ways of pleasantness and their paths were paths of peace; they were honored by others and they were proud of themselves. There is little doubt that so far as the pains and pleasures of human life go they were happy men; but so intent were their minds upon obedience to the rules and regulations of the laws of the kingdom of man that they were not even aware that there was any other kingdom, to say nothing of its laws.

In the midst of such mysteries as lie at the entrance to the way of life all ordinary powers of perception are at fault. It is useless and hopeless to rely upon human understanding when confronted with the unsearchable mysteries of the beginnings of life. Science and philosophy have spent ages past in the endeavor to solve the mystery of the origin of life. But at the close of the nineteenth century, the greatest discoveries of science, and perhaps the grandest generalizations of philosophy have led to the knowledge of—what? In a word, to the knowledge that such things are to the human mind forever unknowable. Religion owes to agnosticism a great debt. Since by no amount of observation can the scientist throw the least gleam of light upon the origin of the life as we see it upon the earth, it is not to be expected that we should understand the origin of the life of heaven. Nicodemus, like many another one, bewildered upon the first growing conviction that a new life must be obtained, strove first to understand the beginnings of it, but this Christ promptly rebuked. The generation of life was no more to be understood than the movements of the wind, yet was none the less real; the generation of the new spirit life is no more to be understood by man than the generation of the new life he sees about him. Guided by the laws of evolution he may go back and back through the modifications of terrestrial life if he choose, but he will at length be confronted with the chasm between the living and the not-living, and this is a chasm not to be bridged by human comprehension; here is a problem not to be solved.

But that life which is in existence, however that existence came about, he sees reproduced, and continued, and passed from the living to the not-living on every hand.

How life came into existence he cannot tell, and why the living generates new lives he knows not nor probably ever will. But that life has come upon the earth he knows, and that living creatures generate new living creatures after their kind he also knows. He knows besides that certain acts or conduct on the part of the living creature are necessary to generate its life in new creatures; only by conforming to fixed and immutable laws is life propagated; only by the proper conduct of the living creature is a new life created. He is able to know what this conduct is, and see its results in the ever-increasing life upon the earth. So that the experience of man gives him some guidance in trying to find the way of the new life. Left to himself indeed, since good conduct and ill as related to the present life seem merged in one as regards their inefficiency in securing the future life, his case might seem hopeless. But since proper conduct leads to the generation of human life and the keeping of it, it is comprehensible to him that the conduct prescribed by Christ may lead to the generation of the new life, although why such conduct should lead to such a result may be wrapped in impenetrable mystery; convinced that his present conduct leads to death, and convinced that there is another life, his mind is at least able to suppose that the conduct prescribed by Christ may lead to the obtaining of this other life. But what is the conduct prescribed by Christ? He declared it in plain terms to Nicodemus in the beginning, and he and his apostles enforced it and re-enforced it throughout their lives. "For God so loved the world that he gave his only begotten Son, that whosoever believeth in him should not perish but have eternal life." That alone is the desired conduct which necessarily permits the communion with the Spirit, which is requisite to the birth of a new spiritual creature; and such conduct is wrapped up in and evolves from faith in Christ and in his teachings. The conduct is simple and easy to be understood; the resulting birth is an inscrutable mystery.

The conversion, the turning from the old way to the new, may, so far as outward appearance goes, be great in some cases and small in others. The new course of conduct prescribed by Christ may seem so nearly parallel to the usual course of one's life as to be impatiently and instantly repudiated. How many an unbeliever, comparing his own course with that of the Christian, is convinced that his own conduct is just as likely, nay even more likely to lead to the kingdom of heaven, if there be one. It is the case of Naaman the Syrian again. Why should bathing in the water of the Jordan produce results different from or even as good as a plunge in the greater rivers of Syria? Mankind is ever prone to look for great causes to produce great effects, and to determinedly refuse to believe that apparently slight differences in conduct may be fraught with the gravest results. People in the midst of a cholera epidemic have determinedly refused to believe that drinking one kind of water rather than another could make any difference, and died in consequence.

The conduct prescribed by Christ is declared by him to be necessary to create within man the character fitted to receive the life-giving influence of the Spirit. There seems to be no doubt in the expressions of Scripture that man has the power to turn into the way of life, to place himself within the range of the life-giving power of the kingdom of God, to enter upon the course of conduct in the first instance which shall place him within the grip of forces which ever after and irresistibly carry him forward in the way of life eternal. In the case of ordinary animals subject to our observation we note that the new creature, once having been created, grows by forces not under its own control, which carry it forward and develop it. It needs only to be placed in conditions congenial for the development of its own peculiar organism, and its own vital forces do the rest. But the generation of a new living organism must be first accomplished, and in that the volition of pre-existing animals is involved. The great difference between the entrance into the animal and into the spiritual kingdom is that the creatures of the animal kingdom have no participation in the acts or conduct leading to their own birth, while in the spiritual kingdom man must himself do that which decides whether or no he will be born again. If he is to obtain an entrance into the spiritual kingdom he must be born again, and also consciously or unconsciously adopt the course of conduct necessary to the new birth.

At birth the human being is endowed with the animal life and the human life by the preexisting living beings having these kinds of life. According to the accepted theology, man is endowed at the same time with spiritual life. But this is not the doctrine taught in the Bible. On the contrary it is stated in the most emphatic terms that the spiritual beings do not propagate their own species, but that every one that enters the realm of spirit life must be born, not only anew, but anew (or from above) of the Spirit. The stream of spiritual life does not pass onward in the same way that we observe it to pass in the various species of the animal life. The horse of to-day is the living embodiment of equine vital forces which had their origin back in geological times. The equine life has flowed on from horse to horse from those distant ages even down to now without a single lapse or break. The same is true of the life of the wheat plant of the present time; it is the present living embodiment of wheat life which has existed on the earth for ages. Man's animal life, too, has been handed down from generation to generation and passed through countless embodiments. And if we accept the teachings of some evolutionists, the life of the man and the horse and (if we go to extremes) even the wheat are mere present exhibitions of a continuous chain of vital forces, the end of which is lost in the molten rocks of the primordial globe. But the Scriptures teach that the spiritual life is not of this sort. The spirit of each being comes to him, not from his human ancestor, but direct from God, and thus do the believers become in very deed the "sons of God." Each human being therefore must preside over his own spiritual birth; he cannot inherit his spirit life from his ancestors; it must be obtained from contact with the living Spirit in each case, and cannot be transmitted. Nor is this contrary to nature, for science teaches that creatures resulting from the union of widely different life-currents are sterile.

The influence of the Spirit is omnipresent, but by the conduct involved in conversion must man's soul be prepared and put in the condition necessary for the generation of the seed of the Spirit and the production of the spiritual organism or new creature. This is not only according to Scripture but according to nature; the conditions under which living creatures may be created and under which they may develop are under the control of man. The vital forces are not his, but the conditions under which they act are in many instances under his control. Living beings come into existence at his will, and according to the conditions which he is able to prescribe they grow and develop or die. Therefore that the creation of the new spiritual creatures should depend upon conditions to be brought about by mankind is in entire accordance with that which is a matter of common knowledge to the meanest of the human species.

It may be noted that the preparations for the propagation and preservation of life in any kingdom are frequently connected with that which is subject to the laws of a lower kingdom. Man prepares a seed-bed in the earth for the reception of the wheat. While there is no life in the seed-bed, upon its proper preparation it depends whether the wheat will ever germinate or no. The living power within the seed cannot produce the living plant unless by means of proper preparation of the seed-bed, the prerequisite conditions of life are called into existence. Looking to the fertilized ovule, we find that the organism evolved is habitually nourished from the elements prepared in a next lower kingdom. The plant lives upon the prepared earthy elements, the animal is nourished by the plant, or another animal which lives upon the plant. The human soul or mind depends upon the body, is so interwoven with it that the existence of the one cannot be separated from the other. Indeed, so intimate is the dependence that the operations of the one might easily be mistaken for the operations of the other. How in accordance with experience, then, to find that the preparation for the generation of the new spirit life, and for its nourishment, is directed to that which affects the soul or mind of man. The whole conduct prescribed by Christ as the prerequisite of the generation of spirit life, and for its nourishment when brought into existence, is such as affects the psychological element of man. If there be a spirit life and it be higher than the human life, higher than the soul life of man, the part of man demanding preparation for its generation and nourishment should be his soul; and so we find it.

CHAPTER VIII

GOD'S SOVEREIGNTY AND MAN'S AGENCY

IN the past chapters God and man have been regarded as co-workers, so to speak, in securing man's entrance into the spiritual kingdom; but this relationship is of such great importance, and has been the subject of so much controversy, that it deserves to be more closely studied. Not only since the dawn of history, but in the twilight of mythology, the human race has worshiped God, has stood in awe of some supernatural power. In some cases the ideas concerning this supernatural power have been crude, even to the point of being grotesque, as viewed from our standpoint of to-day; in other cases they have been wrought into highly developed systems; in some cases they command our admiration for their pure beauty, and in others excite our disgust by their bestial qualities; but in all the belief is firmly held that there is a power superior to the human race, having control of its destinies. This fact of the universal, or wellnigh universal, belief of mankind in a God of some sort has been explained in many ways; the Christian, the pagan and the agnostic philosopher all recognize the existence of a belief in the supernatural, wherever the human race has been found: the explanations vary, but the fact is undisputed.

The Hebrew Scriptures do not attempt to prove, they assert that "in the beginning God created the heavens and the earth," that the earth exhibits the wisdom of God and that the heavens declare his glory. The Hebrew nation was taught to believe in God, not by argument in word but by argument in deed; they were given exhibitions of his power in certain particulars and left to infer it in all particulars; but their belief in a God was not peculiar to them; belief in a supernatural ruler was widespread in their day.

Along with the belief of the peoples in a supernatural being ruling over their fortunes, came a necessary corollary, their resort to prayer and sacrifice, as a manifestation of their inferiority and willingness to obey. The belief of the heathen world was that the power of God would be exerted for or against particular men and nations in accordance with the manifestation to him, by word and deed, of their submission to his authority. As the power was the king's, yet advancement depended upon the conduct of the courtier, so the power resided in God, but the benefits of it could be procured by man, only by imitating the submission, reverence and prayer of the subject. The same doctrine was taught in a thousand varying ways in the Hebrew Scriptures; man was under obligation to acknowledge the Ruling Power of the universe and put himself in subjection to his laws. We need not go further than the Pentateuch to find this lesson inculcated by every use of language and ceremony; and we may go to the end of Hebrew Scriptures and find the changes rung upon this subject in a never-ending variety of lessons. The ceremonies connected with the tabernacle, the laws for regulating civil conduct given by Moses, the wars of the Judges, the elaborate ceremonies of the temple, the words of the prophets, the captivity and return, all are permeated with two complementary lessons—the infinite power of God and man's control over his own destiny. In the conclusion of Deuteronomy we find Moses solemnly declaring, "See I have set before thee this day life and good, and death and evil; in that I command thee this day to love the Lord thy God, to walk in his ways, and to keep his commandments, that thou mayst live and multiply. But if thy heart

GOD'S SOVEREIGNTY

turn away, so that thou wilt not hear, but shall be drawn away, and worship other gods, and serve them, I denounce unto thee this day that ye shall surely perish. . . . I call heaven and earth to witness against you this day, that I have set before thee life and death, the blessing and the curse; therefore choose life." And this sentiment and this farewell declaration of Moses was never departed from or varied by prophet or priest claiming to speak the word of God till prophecy ceased in the land of Israel.

At the time therefore of the coming of Christ, the people who listened to the declarations of John and the discourses of Jesus asked no proof either of the sovereignty of God or man's power to dispose of his own destiny. The contradictory qualities of the two propositions did not seem to exercise the minds of men in those days, they simply accepted both and acted upon them. Then as now there were a few unbelievers in God, but they counted for little amidst the masses of the people. Atheism has never found congenial soil upon the earth, for the ordinary man finds himself and his works subject to a power above him and worships instinctively.

John the Baptist therefore spent no time in persuading the multitudes which came to him that there was a God, or that man needed to obey him if he looked for life; the multitude believed in these things as matters of fact probably as fully as John. But John did address himself to persuading the multitude that they did not understand the law of God, and therefore it was needless to say were not obeying it. They came out to him believing in God, to be sure, but believing also that the children of Abraham, in the flesh, were possessed of a divine patent, so to speak, insuring them a position in the heavenly kingdom. But John said, "Ye offspring of vipers, who warned you to flee from the wrath to come?" What a shock it must have been to these self-satisfied people, who were comforting themselves with the thought that they were children of Abraham, to be addressed as the offspring of vipers. As a basis of hope for escape from destruction they might as well have been broods of detested reptiles as the physical children of Abraham. They were committing the fatal error of supposing that they had inherited from their fathers spiritual, and therefore eternal life. They had yet to learn, what Christ told Nicodemus, that that which is born of the flesh is flesh and that only that which is born of the spirit is spirit. "Bring forth therefore fruits meet for repentance," cried John; do those things which are evidences of the fact that you recognize that you have been in error and have set your faces towards the right goal. So long as they said within themselves, "We have Abraham to our father," and relied upon the inheritance of life by descent from him, they could not inherit it, for they believed that they were in the right way already while in truth they were in the broad road to destruction. But when the truth came home to their intelligence that God the Father of spirits was able of the very stones to raise up children unto Abraham, the conviction would come that they must be up and doing if they would escape the wrath to come. God's power was indeed infinite as both John and they believed; he could raise up children from the very stones. But he did not act arbitrarily and without method comprehensible to man. He had ordained certain uniform laws, to which man could conform and to which he must conform or be lost. The multitude had no difficulty in understanding John's point at the conclusion of his discourse. They said, "What must we do?" John was practical, and as the question to him was what must we do, he prescribed deeds, he dwelt not so much upon "why" as upon "what." His hearers could not practice what

John preached without becoming in kind what John was. Those who followed John prepared themselves for Jesus. No one can read the few brief texts of John's discourse and not be struck with their Christlike character. John came only to prepare; he with the baptism of water made clean the soul to receive the spark of life from the Holy Spirit. John baptized with water, but Christ with the Holy Ghost and with fire. Those who received the baptism of the Holy Spirit would be as safe as the wheat gathered into the garner, but those who repented not nor turned from the way they were in would be as surely and completely destroyed as the chaff would be by an unquenchable fire. So John departed not from the principles of Moses and the prophets. The power of God and the will of man needed to join hands to secure life. As Moses declared God's power and yet left the choice between life and death with man himself, so John, first declaring the unlimited power of God, laid upon each man's shoulders the burden of his own salvation. This do, and ye shall live, was the declaration of Moses; John's proclamation was—bring forth fruits. So at the very beginning and the very end of the Mosaic dispensation it was not left in doubt that man himself determined between life and death. From Moses to John there is not the faintest intimation that man's destiny did not depend upon his own will.

Did Christ reverse the long line of precedent? Not by any means; we have his own declaration that he came not to destroy but to fulfill; not even one jot or tittle was to be altered. His doctrine was the very development of the principles of the law and the prophets. He neither detracted from the infinite power of God declared in the Scriptures, nor on the other hand did he molest in the slightest particular the oft-declared responsibility of man for his own destiny. The people bitten by the serpents in the wilderness were as good as dead from the instant the bite was received; an element was in their blood which left to itself worked out death. Moses prayed unto the Lord for salvation of the people, not doubting that the power to save must come from God. But so necessary does it seem to have been to enforce upon the minds of the people that though salvation come from the Lord it must come by virtue of their own action, that Moses was directed to erect the brazen serpent, at which the stricken people must gaze in order to remain in the land of the living. They themselves were obliged to do something for themselves or die. Christ seized upon this, to Nicodemus, well-known incident to force home upon his confused mind the all-important lesson, saying to him "As Moses lifted up the serpent in the wilderness, even so must the Son of man be lifted up, that whosoever believeth in him should not perish but have eternal life." Not all the stricken Israelites received life, only those who were willing to turn towards the brazen serpent; not all the children of Abraham should have eternal life, but only those who turned to Christ, only those who confided in him, trusted to him, and yielded up their own ways to follow his. As the serpent was a needful object-lesson in the wilderness, so was the Son of man the needed object-lesson to mankind. Those who turn are saved; those who refuse pass on to destruction. "He that believeth on the Son hath eternal life, but he that obeyeth not the Son shall not see life, but the wrath of God abideth on him." As with Moses and the prophets and as with John the Baptist, so with Christ, the believing still involves obedience, obedience to the law of the kingdom which one wishes to enter and in which he desires to abide. The obedience to the laws of the human kingdom is sufficient for that kingdom, but fails to produce an entrance into the higher kingdom. Those that obey not the Son shall not see life; they shall not lose it, they shall never obtain it.

Running through all the words of Christ and his apostles like warp and woof were the two great doctrines of the sovereignty of God and the free will of man. These things were not explained but asserted. It must not be forgotten that the very early Church had the tremendous force and influence behind it of Christ's recent personal presence upon earth. It is hard to realize the greatness of this power. In those very early days, statement, assertion and exhortation, and not argument, were the useful weapons of the Church. The Church as time went on lost this advantage, but gained the equivalent one of the power of history. The fulfillment in these days has as great weight and authority with mankind as the announcement in the days of Christ. But as time went on, believers were obliged to give a reason for the hope which was within them; to declaration and exhortation had to be added argument. The introduction of a new antagonistic and exclusive religion by peaceful means demanded of necessity, argument and explanation: the apostles themselves set the example. They found both with the Jew and Greek the necessity of argument; with the Jew to show that Christianity was the fulfillment of the law; with the Greek to show that it was not antagonistic to the nature of things. Since Christians were precluded from spreading their religion by the sword, they were driven to convince by reasoning.

Moreover, Christianity made theology a concern of the people. Whatever philosophers may have done before the advent of Christianity, the people had not concerned themselves with theology. The very proselyting by the innumerable Christian missionaries bred argument among the people. Paul and his followers asked only the privilege of addressing the people. The people not only questioned the missionaries, but themselves began theorizing to explain how these things could be. Before the days of the apostles were concluded we find this great discussion of religion productive not only of incalculable good, but also of no little evil. Paul and the other writers found it necessary to combat many wrong theories, because wrong theory soon brought in its train wrong practice. Where wrong theories were allowed to breed unhindered, the Church was speedily destroyed. The need of explanation and expounding the new religion was as manifest as the need of sunlight, but the best-intentioned expounders now and again drifted into vagaries which could not be defended. But worse than this, a spirit grew up in the Church, or at least among some of the great leaders of the Church, that religion must be reduced to a system which should leave nothing further to be explained. The doctrines so plainly enunciated in the Old Testament, so explicitly declared by Christ and his apostles, God's sovereignty and man's free will, could not long escape the attention of the systematizers. In practice these two doctrines got along very harmoniously together, but in theory they troubled the Church greatly. It seems so plain that these two doctrines should stand together that it is hard to conceive why Christians, from the time of the Church Fathers until now, have been so determined to subordinate the one to the other, or rather exclude one by the other, unless it be that they have been unable to withstand the taunts of the infidel that their religion contained a staring, irreconcilable contradiction. The controversy in the Church over this matter waxed greater and greater, until it ended in the turbulent contentions in the days of Athanasius and Arius, when mingled words and cudgels were used in Church councils, and armed men determined decisions. Athanasius may be said to have prevailed in establishing in the Western Church the doctrine that man's salvation is the work of God alone. Later on the great authority of Augustine was exercised in favor of the doctrine that God determined salvation to the entire exclusion of man's agency in the matter. Calvin in the Protestant Church reduced this doctrine to the plainest and most undisguised formula when he declared his famous doctrine of predestination. But from the time of Arius, whether under the name of synergism, that is to say the co-working of God and man, or semipelagianism, or Arminianism, the scriptural doctrine that man had a voice in his own destiny has survived in the Church. Not even the great authority of Athanasius, Augustine and Calvin, than whom no greater minds ever existed in the Church, has sufficed to keep the great body of Christians to the doctrine that God has irrevocably appointed man to salvation or damnation without any agency of man in the matter.

Forgetting that nature has always refused to be conformed to any exact system, that it is complicated beyond any power of classification, man is ever struggling to reduce all things to what he considers order. So long as it is thoroughly realized that the insolvable lies ever beyond the last solved, and that

GOD'S SOVEREIGNTY

knowledge is bounded on every hand by the unknown, and that the explanation will always need to be explained, this is proper and necessary to all progress. With this realization before us, let us approach the doctrines of predestination and free will.

The arguments to prove that God must foreknow all things are unanswerable. Having arrived at this stage in the argument, it seems a playing with words to deny that God must have foreordained all that has come about or will come about, including the salvation or damnation of every particular human being. On this battleground the Calvinist easily puts to rout his opponents. He has undeniable premises and reaches his conclusions by impregnable logic. Did he but stop there, no fault could be found with his doctrine, but when he goes one step further and says, in the words of the Confession of Faith, that man's salvation is "out of God's mere free grace and love, without any foresight of faith or good works or perseverance in either of them or any other thing in the creature, as conditions or causes moving him thereunto," and that "Man, by his fall into a state of sin, hath wholly lost all ability of will to any spiritual good accompanying salvation; so as a natural man being altogether averse to that good, and dead in sin, is not able, by his own strength to convert himself or prepare himself thereunto," he not only antagonizes the innate feelings of mankind, but goes counter to the plain statements of the Scriptures. "Strive to make your calling and election sure," is as much Scripture as "By grace alone are ye saved." The Calvinist places great reliance upon the saying of Christ that no man can come unto him except the Father draw him. There is no disposition to controvert or to qualify this bald statement. It expresses the truth and sets forth the controlling power of God in his universe, as unqualifiedly as any Augustinian or Calvinist could possibly desire. Yet this power of God is exercised, to quote from the Confession of Faith, "So as thereby neither is God the author of sin, nor is violence offered to the will of the creature, nor is the liberty or contingency of second causes taken away, but rather established." Once more, if Calvinism had made this statement of man's agency a fundamental element of its doctrine, no fault could be found with its position on this matter. But then there would have been no Calvinism as plain people understand what is meant by that term. It is because Calvinism is unwilling to allow God's sovereignty and man's agency both to stand that it has created such antagonism. But to take out this distinctive feature would be to destroy the thing itself. Calvinism is unwilling to allow the two doctrines to remain in its system without harmonizing them, and its manner of creating harmony is to cause the one doctrine to reduce the other to mere words without force or comprehensible meaning. Let us see if with the added light of the works of God, which the race enjoys to-day, these seeming contradictions of his word can be harmonized without doing violence to either.

CHAPTER IX

CAUSE

THE modern investigation of natural forces leads to the conclusion that no unit of force is ever lost, that matter is never destroyed. Every manifestation of force is merely bringing under our notice something which existed before and will continue to exist hereafter. Nothing can occur which is not the result of some previous occurrence or combination of occurrences; and nothing can occur without itself being in turn the cause of subsequent occurrences, and so on *ad infinitum.*

The single autumn leaf which is now twirling and fluttering to the ground is the result of causes which were at work before the dawn of life upon the earth. The puff of air which was the final determining cause of its fall at the particular moment, is the result of a complicated series of events, stretching back into past ages, until even the imagination of man can follow them no longer. The air with its oxygen and nitrogen and carbon was compounded, one dares not state how long since.

It was a part of the sun once; then certain events determined that the atoms of gas which form the breeze moving against the leaf, should not be thrown off to become a part of Neptune or Jupiter, but should be thrown off to become a part of the Earth. Other causes determined that this particular oxygen should not become united with a part of the solid crust of the earth to form its sand or its clay but should remain free in the atmosphere. The presence of the elements in the atmosphere having been thus determined by far-off causes, the mind is bewildered in contemplating the thousand thousand causes which have acted upon the particles of oxygen and nitrogen and carbon of the air which blew down the leaf. How many myriads of times those particles may have gone in and out of living plants and animals and been carried hither and thither over the face of the earth; and while a part of the atmosphere, what world-encircling journeys may they have made during the ages since the earth had an atmosphere; how many times may they have blown in the steady trade-winds of the tropics, or have been whirled in cyclones over land and sea, now taking part in scarcely moving breezes and again assisting in terrific gales, now sent up by the heated earth to the upper regions of the air, and now sent down heavy and cold to the earth again. Hither and thither they have gone, through countless ages, urged on by an infinity of complicated causes, until at length they have moved against the face of the just ripened leaf and caused its fall. But the puff of air against the leaf was only the last link in the chain ending in the immediate cause of the leaf's fall. Some man mayhap planted the tree. Who shall attempt to run back the cause upon cause and series of causes which brought that particular man to that particular part of the earth; what teeming events in the life of each of his ancestors, each contributing in the end to the man being at the required place. The tree being planted, how many causes conspired to produce the growth of the tree, enabled it to resist the attacks of insects, caused it to survive the drought of summer and the cold of winter. Then in the production of the tree branch by branch and twig upon twig, until the bud of this particular leaf was formed, how many causes were at work to bring thither all the atoms of carbon and oxygen and nitrogen and potash and other elements of the tree to the required spot. And then how many agencies were brought to bear to produce the ripened leaf, at the particular time when the extra force of the particular air had strength enough to carry it from its branch. This glimpse of a few of the causes of one leaf's fall shows their complication to be beyond the comprehension of any save an infinite intelligence. But nevertheless the leaf has fallen, the event has taken place by virtue of other events spreading abroad in every direction of space and extending back in time to where they are lost in the confines of eternity.

Science likewise renders it sure and certain that the falling of even one leaf produces effects which have never an end in producing other effects. One cannot remember a single event which has not been produced by some other event or combination of events; and these of course were likewise produced by some cause. Every event therefore becomes a cause to some subsequent event, and every cause was beforetime an effect. The movement of the locomotive along its track, and sailing of the steamship across the ocean, are partly caused by the events of the carboniferous age, when the luxuriant forests grew and decayed, and were then packed in sand and clay, to await, in the after ages, the exploring pick and candle of the miner. What countless other causes have come moving through the ages to bring about the sailing of a particular ship from its port on a certain day and hour; and yet they come on with the precision of a well-trained army concentrating upon an objective point. If any one of ten thousand different occurrences had been different that ship had not sailed at that time; but they were not different, they were precisely as they were, and therefore the ship sailed. Even in society, whose occurrences have been so complicated and confusing that even now it is disputed if there be a science of sociology, the chains of causes are seen at work. We see dimly, to be sure, but still we see how the events of history are brought about by causes no less certain, although harder to observe, than in the departments of physical science. So it is seen that nothing occurs to-day that does not arise from a concentration of causes at the particular time and place, which had their beginnings in ages past. Unless we dare deny the law that every effect has a cause, there seems no escape from the conclusion that every event of to-day is the legitimate, inexorable outcome of causes which began to work before the earth was born or ever the heavens were formed.

One thing is the effect of some other thing,

when that which we call the effect not only invariably does follow that which we know as the cause, but must follow it. The paling of the stars invariably precedes the rising of the sun, but the paling of the stars is not the cause of the rising of the sun, because there is no necessity in this sequence of events, there is no necessary connection between the two. The facts that the stars pale before a brilliant display of the aurora borealis or in the presence of the full moon, that the revolution of the earth on its axis involves the rising of the sun, and many others which will readily suggest themselves, tend to prove that the paling of the stars is not a necessary precedent to the rising of the sun. Had we no further knowledge on the subject than that the stars invariably first paled and then the sun rose, we would be justified in believing the one to be the cause of the other. Many a grave error in human affairs has been made because lack of knowledge has prevented people from knowing that apparently invariably preceding things were not causes of the events which apparently invariably happened after them, because the element of necessity was absent. In determining what preceding events are the cause of following events the human observer is also hampered by the unavoidable difficulty of not knowing whether those things which seem invariably to precede other things and therefore are their cause, in reality do invariably so precede them.

Two questions arise to disturb the inference of the invariable precedence of one of two given events by the other: first, whether during intervals when the given occurrences were not under observation they preceded and followed one another, as when under observation before and after the intervals; and secondly, if the observation has been continuous for a certain length of time, whether before and after the period of observation the given events occurred in the same order as during the time of observation. This difficulty is one of the negative strongholds of those evolutionists who contend that at some time in ages past the living spontaneously evolved from the not-living. Recognizing the indisputable fact that no such thing as spontaneous generation exists in the world as we know it to-day, their reply is that it cannot be said that the order of events which we observe to-day in this matter has always existed. At the present time we say that all life is caused by some preceding life, that is to say that a living organism is the invariable and necessary precedent of new life. Life has been demonstrated to invariably precede new life, and we conclude that it is necessary because no amount of observation or experiment has ever disclosed life following any other thing, when pre-existing life was absent. But of course the invariability and the necessity are both inferences from our experience, or from the experience of those who have preceded us; and while this experience amounts to that which we know as moral certainty, it, in the nature of things, can never amount to demonstration. Therefore the strict evolutionist who holds to the theory that everything now visible has been evolved out of the primordial star-mist, without any special creation at any period of the history of the globe, cannot be contradicted when he declares that while all life is now caused by pre-existing life, this may not always have been so, since at some period what we now observe to be the invariable and necessary precedent of life may not then have been either invariable or necessary.

Our knowledge of cause and effect is then bounded by our experience, which enables us to say what events invariably and necessarily precede and follow other events. Our confidence in certain events which we call causes producing certain events which we call effects, is proportioned to our experience rendering more or less certain whether the two given events invariably and necessarily precede and follow each other, and to our inability, as a result of our experience, to disassociate the one from the other, or to conceive of the one happening without the other. The hunter relies with every confidence upon killing the oncoming lion by a bullet through the heart, because the cumulative experience of the human race has been that the piercing of the heart is invariably and necessarily followed by death.

Of the underlying nature of the relation between cause and effect we know very little. That the one follows the other invariably and necessarily is about the sum-total of our real knowledge. If, while we explain why the piercing of the heart produces death and the piercing of the arm does not, we note the explanation, we shall see that after all what we have done is only to show, first, that the pierced heart or arm is followed by certain other occurrences, and these occurrences by others, and that death follows as the end of the series of events in one case and not in the other; and secondly, that we cannot conceive of a pierced heart disassociated with death. When it comes to the actions of certain poisons we are at a perfect loss to say why the introduction of these substances into the animal system is fatal in its consequences. Poisons producing death, which leave behind no visible effects of their presence, we call obscure causes, merely meaning thereby that we are unable to detect occurrences following their introduction into the animal system, which we have been commonly in the habit of finding preceding death.

Knowing therefore that every event must be caused by preceding, and must itself be the cause of following events; and realizing that cause is merely the thing invariably and necessarily preceding some other thing which is called the effect; and further realizing that our knowledge of cause and effect is gathered from and limited by our range of observation and experience, we are led to the unavoidable conclusion that an infinite being, knowing at any particular points the events then occurring, must of necessity know with absolute certainty that other events must necessarily follow them, and then what events must follow these, and so on down through the ages into eternity future. Because the connection between cause, that is the preceding event, and effect, that is the following event is, as has been seen, invariable and necessary, the causing event must always and ever bring after it the effect; the one is inseverably linked to the other. Cause and effect are like an endless chain; when one link is drawn every succeeding link follows as a matter of course; only in the chain of events there is never a break. The chain was forged by an infinite power, and a break is as inconceivable as a breach in the continuity of space. We see a portion of the chain passing before us; on the one hand it is being drawn into eternity past, and on the other it is being drawn out of eternity future. Thus to an infinite intelligence there can be no such thing as past, present or future, as the ideas present themselves to the human mind. That which has been and that which shall be is as certain and present as that which is.

So long as the causes are not too much complicated with other causes, man himself has no difficulty in foreknowing. The motions and positions of the heavenly bodies are foreknown with great certainty and for long periods of time, because the necessary and invariable sequence of events is comparatively simple. But one force is acting powerfully, and man's experience has taught him what the causes of the varying positions are, that is to say he has learned what is the invariable necessary precedence and sequence of events in this limited field of occurrences. In gunnery the track and striking place of the projectile are most accurately predicted and calculated upon. Engineers have no difficulty in calculating, in advance of a single stone being laid or a single rod placed in the structure of a bridge, just what span is necessary and what weight can be carried. The chemist is able in advance to say what effects will follow the mixture of certain elements; that is to say he not only can predict but he can foreordain with a certain degree of precision what shall result, for example, from the ignition of certain quantities of oxygen and hydrogen. In the more complicated sequences in social and political life man also exhibits his power of foreknowledge and predestination. In this he certainly exhibits the truth that he was created in the image of God. Every able statesman, general and business man is continually ordering the events of the future by his knowledge of the past and present. Given the knowledge of certain moving events, and these men predict the events of the future; and by their own efforts and dispositions they themselves bring about with a considerable degree of certainty things future. Man is of course limited in his ability to predict the future by lack of knowledge; and when the event has disappointed the diplomat or general he is frequently able to see why he failed, and his regret is intensified by the fact that lack of knowing something which might have been known has caused a fatal miscarriage.

In illustrating the nature of cause and effect, single chains of events have been taken for the sake of illustration. Of course nature and the affairs of men offer no such single chains of events; every event brings in its train more than one other event, and when the events are numerous the following events are in proportion. It is difficult to trace the effects of any given force, since no force is acting alone. There are always forces acting simultaneously, partly neutralizing, partly fortifying each other. The effects of single forces can only be arrived at inferentially, and by making allowance for the action of other forces in the produced events. All experiments upon the force of gravity are disturbed by the force exercised by the resisting air. The actual path of the projectile from the cannon is the result of not only the force of the explosive, but the force of gravity and the resistance of the air. The force of the explosive therefore can only be computed by allowing for the parts played by the other forces which go to produce the actual event. Therefore it is that certain events, which if existing without concurring events would be followed by certain effects, are not so followed; because there is a concurrence of causes or forces, and the effect is the resultant of their union. As the concurring events or causes multiply it becomes more and more difficult to calculate the effect which any one would have produced if acting alone. Therefore even when all the causes are known it becomes more and more difficult, as they increase, to predict what their united result will be. The difficulty is increased if the relative intensity or power of each is not known at all or only guessed at. And of course the difficulty is once more vastly increased in those cases where only a part of the concurring events or causes is known. Thus the difficulties increase, until at last prediction becomes an impossibility, and the future becomes proverbially uncertain. In the social and moral world, man stands well-nigh but not quite powerless to predict the future, because of the multiplicity and variety of events, the impossibility of measuring the relative power of each, and his ability to note but few of them at a time. Nevertheless, even in society enough is observed to render it certain that the same inexorable sequences of events occur as in more readily observed departments of knowledge; and the best observers are thoroughly convinced that it is only the complexity of the problem that prevents the solution, that a sufficiency of knowledge would enable the future history of political bodies to be as accurately predicted as eclipses of the sun.

But in God of course there can be no lack of knowledge, and therefore no limit to the extent of his power to foreknow every future event as the necessary outcome of those which went before it. And since infinite power must be as certainly predicated of God as infinite knowledge, and since it would be absurd to withhold from God a power of which we see the rudiments in man, we must suppose that God produces events, and that these events in their turn produce with certainty other events, as we have seen. And we must further credit God with what the civil law insists on crediting man—although in man's case it often does not hold good—the intending of the natural results of his actions. So then what is passing to-day and that which shall come to pass must have been foreknown and intended and foreordained by the Creator and Governor of the universe. Science fortifies the doctrine deduced by the Westminster divines from the Scriptures. But what has become of man's free will? Let us investigate this branch of the subject.

CHAPTER X

FREE WILL

It is owing to this connection between event and event that the evolutionist is able to trace the history of the earth and the life upon it. Starting with the early existence of life upon the earth, without inquiring how it began, evolution shows a development of life by the action of the forces of the environment, assisted by nothing within the organism higher than unconscious reflex action. But there would seem to have come a time when the further advance in quality of life and grade of living creature demanded a new instrument of development. The plants and the lower animals had improved by virtue of the various influences of their habitat, acting in conjunction with the unconscious, non-intelligent changes within themselves; but a large factor in the evolution of the higher species of animals has been the exercise of intelligence by individuals. Darwin's theory of natural selection beautifully explains many mysteries of the progress of life; with its shortcomings we have now nothing to do. To his doctrine of natural selection, finding it incapable of explaining many observed facts, he added the further doctrine of sexual selection, which just as beautifully explains further mysteries. He shows that many more individuals of a species are created than the habitat of the species is able to support or the enemies of the species permit to survive. He shows further that those individuals of the species possessing variations rendering the obtaining of food or the escape from enemies more easy, tend to survive, while the less fortunate members of the species perish; that these variations are transmitted to progeny; and that therefore by this survival of the fittest the species improves, until it arrives at the highest attainable adaptability to its surroundings and becomes as perfect as its circumstances will allow. Mr. Darwin further shows that in the meeting between the sexes the individuals select those who are most pleasing, and that the beauties of animals and birds are largely due to the selection by birds and beasts of mates most gratifying to each other in attractive features.

In the plant kingdom the working of the principle of natural selection depends upon what we might call the blind agencies like heat and moisture and soil and enemies of various sorts, acting to preserve the better adapted and to destroy the less adapted; and since the tendency of plants and animals alike is to produce after their kind, the fittest not only survive in their own generation, but propagate those best fitted to survive in the next. But in the animal kingdom the element of choice is introduced; and whether relying upon natural selection or sexual selection to show the development of the animal kingdom, Mr. Darwin continually calls attention to the intelligent conduct of the individuals themselves. It is true, to be sure, that the various incident forces acting upon the species conspire to cause the survival of the best equipped individuals, without any voluntary action on the part of the individual. Weapons of offence and defence were developed in this manner. The carnivorous animal with the best teeth and the best claws had better chances of survival than those less well equipped in these particulars. The defensive armor of turtles, crocodiles and porcupines tended to improve by natural selection without any intelligent assistance from the animals themselves; the less securely covered would more readily fall a prey to enemies and be destroyed than those whose armor was more perfect. But in a vast number of instances the progress and perfection of the species could only be attained through the voluntary actions of the individual, all of which involve the power of choosing. The development of the courage of the lion, the craftiness of the fox, the timidity of the hare, and the various mental qualities of the different species of animals, so necessary to their success in life, has depended upon the intelligent response of the animal to its surroundings. The more courageous and crafty carnivora would attack and succeed in gaining food and plenty of it where more cowardly and less resourceful members would perish for lack of it. The scarcity of prey, which would weed out the majority of a generation of animals, would leave surviving those whose ingenuity and daring surmounted the difficulties of obtaining it. The antelopes and deer whose better hearing gave notice of approaching danger, and those whose fleetness of foot gave better chances of escape from it, would be successful in using these advantages in the struggle for life in proportion to their mental acuteness in the use of them; the appreciation of certain sounds would be useless without the quick determination to flee. In the struggle for existence among the animals, life depending, as it does, so largely upon food and drink, the length of life would also depend, in a large measure, upon the exercise of voluntary powers in the search of these. Then too the timely choice of a fit abode, temporary or permanent, would preserve many a flock or herd or solitary animal, whilst those animals whose power of rightly choosing was less largely developed would perish.

Therefore it is seen that the play of the incident forces of nature upon a higher species would have little possibility of improving it in the required direction, under the doctrine of natural selection, were it not for these forces having the power of choice to act upon. The power of choice in the deer to run or stand, the power of choice in the tiger to charge or skulk, have been necessary elements in the production of that timidity in the one and that courage in the other which so essentially characterizes the species as we find them to-day. The mental characteristics in all the higher animals are as necessary parts of their being as teeth and claws. Their obtaining the food and shelter necessary to their own existence, and the rearing of their young, upon which the existence of their species depends, is as dependent upon their dispositions as upon their bones or muscles.

Were the courage and timidity of the deer and the tiger mutually transferred, so that the tiger was ever ready to flee and the deer ever ready to fight, both would speedily be destroyed; the tiger because it would not dare attack the game necessary for its subsistence, and the deer because its courage would lead it into dangers which it had no efficient means to successfully encounter. The forces which, acting upon animal intelligence and power of choice, have, by natural selection and transmission of acquired traits, produced the highly developed animal species of the present age, would have been without any effect whatsoever in such cases had they found nothing to act upon except the unconscious and the non-intelligent. The house-building beaver, the honey-storing bee, the burrowing mole, the flesh-eating lion and the grass-eating ox could never have developed from and become differentiated from the common stock without their endowment of freedom of choice, without which the necessary correspondence between the organism and the environment could not exist.

Certainly no one will deny that freedom of choice to mankind which exists so universally in the higher animals; nor can it be doubted that in the development of man, freedom of choice has been as powerful and as necessary an element as it has been in the animals below him. It is a part of the common experience of every person that his life has been full of "partings of the ways"; and it has been no less a matter of experience how the exercise of choice has been a dominant factor in the development of his character and in determining the progress and outcome of his life. Many choosings have apparently made but little difference; but it must be a person low down in the human scale and of very immature years who cannot look back and locate choosings which have powerfully affected his present character and estate. From the time the child begins to take note of its surroundings, the chief method of controlling its actions is the creation of surroundings calculated to influence choice. Rewards are placed ahead of it in the direction it is desired to pursue, and punishments placed on either hand. At home and in school the same method is pursued, actual physical compulsion being rarely resorted to. Choice is relied upon to develop the child in the required direction. Civil government is founded upon the same system. In rare instances actual physical restraint or compulsion is resorted to; but for the regulation of the vast and complicated affairs of state the voluntary choice of the citizen is depended upon. The whole policy, almost, of society is addressed to the choice of its members. Every election illustrates the point: the electors are persuaded this way and that, and upon the result of the persuasion depends the future policy of the government in this direction and in that. The written laws likewise address themselves to the judgment, patriotism and morality of the people, it being assumed as a necessary postulate of civilized government that the people will choose that which is wise, loyal and just. Without this freedom of choice no progress has ever been made in civilization and in systems of government. Even under the most arbitrary of tyrants the reliance must even yet be upon the power of choosing inherent in the human race. Of what avail the punishment of the disobedient or the reward of the subservient if neither in the one case the subject would choose to escape pain, nor in the other choose to obtain a reward.

But descending to the races having but the rudiments of government, we find still abiding the same freedom of will as a condition, not of progress merely, but of their existence. The very forces of nature surround the lowest savages with choice-compelling situations.

The struggle for existence teaches the lowest human intelligence the advantages of co-operation, whether it be for the purpose of securing adequate shelter, the running down of sufficient game, or the providing of efficient means of protection against enemies. Those who choose to co-operate with each other, yielding a measure of absolute personal freedom for a commensurate advantage in the struggle for life, tend to survive; and those who do not so choose either perish or remain in the lowest state. And if it be possible to conceive of a solitary savage shunning the society of his fellows, even he is not able to flee from the power of choice within him, any more than he would be able to get rid of his shadow. He must choose to hunt when the conditions are favorable, and to prepare for the day of scarcity, or perish from the earth. He must decide between *pros* and *cons* of conduct, as surely and as certainly as his most civilized relation.

As in all grades of civilization so in all occupations, development and choice go hand-in-hand, whether it be in war, diplomacy, business or science. It is a matter of experience that from the time we begin to think we begin to choose; that every act of our lives has in it an element of choice, upon the exercise of which await proportionate success and failure, progress and retrogression.

But with all this choosing there is an inseparable correlative. As vision presupposes an eye, and likewise as necessarily presupposes objects of vision, so choice not only presupposes choosing, but objects of choice. While no man can rid himself of the power of choosing nor of the necessity of exercising it, his choice depends upon the objects presented to it; no man can choose what he has not been made conscious of; he cannot accept what is not offered; he cannot grasp that which is beyond his reach. The present condition of any individual is the result undoubtedly of his choosing, but none the less is it also the result of what from time to time have, with him, been objects of choice. He has been free to do either this or that or the other thing according to the circumstances at the time surrounding him; he was free to choose from those things then presented. From time to time two or more ways were presented and he could pursue any of those at the time open. So that at the end of his course he finds himself in a situation compounded and re-compounded of *choice* and *opportunity*: and these two have ever created each other; opportunities have both limited and compelled choice, and choice has developed opportunities. It is like wind and helm determining from day to day the position of the ship; the one is from within and the other from without. As the wind from time to time seems to place at defiance the power of the helm to vary the course of the ship, so the environment of man seems now and again almost to deprive him of choice; the power of circumstances is so strong as to indicate almost to the point of determination the course that must be pursued. But even in these rare instances there still remains an element of choice. The mariner may conclude that running before the wind is so full of hazard that he may choose to attempt to bring his ship up into the wind even at the risk of foundering, and may founder in consequence of his choice; or he may choose the running as being the less dangerous; but in either case he chooses. So man may turn in the face of the most adverse circumstances, at the risk and even the expense of death itself, or he may allow himself to drift or be driven; but choice is never absent. The situation where circumstances take away the power of choice is inconceivable.

So man's fate must ever depend upon the two co-ordinate forces of free will and environment; and it cannot with truth be said that either one alone has determined his condition. If it cannot be said that he is the creature of circumstances, neither can it be said that he alone controls his course. For not only is his choice limited by the objects presented to it, but the objects also themselves control to a degree the choice. The thief who finds upon one side of him a pointed pistol and on the other an open door, must be admitted to have his choice of the open door controlled by his surrounding circumstances; and so in many another less easily analyzed situation in which man finds himself. In fact, as before indicated, when speaking of the development of children and the government of mankind, the circumstances are very frequently largely determinative of the choice. Men choose just the same, and must choose, but such inducements may be presented on the one side and such deterrents on the other that the choice is controlled by the objects presented. When Moses presented to the children of Israel life and death, blessing and cursing, the intention was of course that the former terms of these pairs of objects should be chosen. Nevertheless, as the future proved, many chose death and not life, cursing and not blessing, thus showing the determinative quality of the choosing of man in spite of the most controlling nature of the objects of choice presented.

But since all the children of Israel had the same choice presented to them at the same time, and some chose death and others chose life, we must seek a further determining factor of man's lot besides the objects of choice and the power of choosing. This further factor is found in the disposition of the mind to which the objects are presented. The hen and the duck upon being placed upon the edge of a pond undoubtedly have the power of choosing to enter the water or remain upon the bank. The objects of choice are the same and the power of choosing is present in both birds. The choice is different because of the difference in disposition of the two birds. The opportunity to walk with its master will be eagerly embraced by the dog and quietly refused by the cat. Each chooses according to its inherent disposition. Nevertheless cats, in exceptional cases, by training, have so had their dispositions altered that they will follow persons to whom they are particularly attached, through fields and gardens " just like dogs," thus showing how disposition controls choice. Among men we find the same rule holding good. It may be predicted in advance that certain races will select stuffs for their personal adornment of the most brilliant and glaring colors, which, presented to the refined taste of cultivated persons, would be rejected. Among certain people polygamy is chosen as an honorable estate for man and not derogatory to women; among other peoples it is not only a crime upon the statute-books, but a state viewed with abhorrence and disgust by man and woman alike. It could therefore be safely predicted that an offer to enter the Sultan's harem, which would be accepted with delight by almost any woman of Constantinople, would be rejected with indignation by almost any woman of London. Things which are eagerly sought after by a man in his youth possess for him no powers of attraction years later; opportunities for them would be therefore as eagerly sought at one time as they would be disdainfully rejected at another. But every one can multiply examples out of his own experience by the score. The powerful influence of disposition upon choice is a matter of common daily experience. But no less certain is it that disposition is itself the creature of choosing; if disposition controls choice, so in turn does choice mold disposition. The effect of choosing certain things or certain kinds of conduct has the effect upon the person choosing of influencing him to choose similarly again. Under the all-powerful influence of countless daily choosings against its promptings, the excitable dispositions become calm, the rash careful, the cruel gentle, and the cowardly brave; and on the contrary every trait is strengthened and confirmed by each choice to follow its dictates.

So man starts in life endowed with this subtle yet supreme power of choice, which nothing can conquer or take away; but he also starts with a twofold environment of physical objects and psychological disposition. Upon this environment depends largely not only what man does, but what he is, so powerful is its influence upon him. But strangely enough, man through choice can and does act so powerfully upon his environment as to almost at times create it, so that what molds man and controls him he himself is to the same extent the creator of.

Through all this action and reaction between man and his environment, determining the eventual characteristics of both man and his environment, we see the necessary part played by free will. Is man to be directed this way or that by external circumstances?

Then the inducements must be made greater and greater upon the one side, and the inconveniences and pains greater and greater on the other side till he chooses to move. Circumstances may control man, but only by acting through his power of choice. Man's disposition, inherited or acquired, may powerfully determine his course this way or that, but again it will be by the influence of this disposition acting through his power of choice. Alternatives will meet him every moment of his conscious existence, and by sheer force of necessity he must choose the one and reject the other. His disposition may and will powerfully influence this choice, even in some cases almost to the point of determination, but it will still remain an influence upon choice and nothing else; the power to choose remains an unaffected reality.

But it may be objected that since circumstances and disposition may exercise a controlling influence upon man's choice, it *amounts* to the same thing as though he enjoyed no choice at all. That it *is* not the same thing we have already seen; man can choose, he does choose, nay more, he must choose. Neither does it amount to the same thing, because, being possessed of the power of choice, and being unable to be deprived of it either by forces without or impulses within, man is always possessed of the means of improvement, however weighted down by his circumstances or hampered by disposition. Because environment is only partially of his own creation, only partially under his control, powers without himself may bring greater and greater influences to bear upon his power of choice, until the changed environment, changed mayhap in spite of himself, may overcome the adverse influence of his own disposition, until he will make a choice looking towards his elevation. And this choosing, as has been seen, may be capable of so acting upon his disposition that a new series of actions and reactions between the man and his environment will take place, in the direction of a better state, until at length the old disposition and its effects will be reduced to infinitesimal proportions, and each stage of growth towards the good be but a preparation for things still better. Man's free will being a possession of which he can be despoiled neither by himself nor another, he can never be deprived of the power of responding to aid from without when it arrives. There is no such thing as the garrison having capitulated and the citadel being in the hands of the enemy when the relieving force has arrived. Upon contemplation it is apparent that the importance of this indestructible quality of man's power of choice cannot be overestimated. It not only is capable of saving him from the evil influences of his external environment, but enables him to be saved from himself.

The view here presented involves the recognition of the importance of the factors of heredity, early training and the surroundings of youth, as fully as the practical experience of mankind compels their recognition. These factors are observed to have such a powerful influence over the lives of men that they form an important basis of action for all mankind. In spite of many exceptions and passages of individuals from one to the other, the ranks of society are preserved almost intact from generation to generation. The training of youths in certain directions is recognized as controlling in a large measure their future destinies; and the results of the vast majority of cases justify the expectations. The Mosaic law did but declare what all men can deduce from experience, when it was stated that God visited the sins of the fathers upon the children unto the third and fourth generation; and all races of men from the savage to the civilized have inculcated with infinite pains the desired lessons in the rising generations.

Thus certain powerful influences upon choice are given at the start and the individual's life given its direction. In society as in physics a body in motion tends to move onward forever in a straight line; and the more powerful the early impulse, whether from disposition or circumstances, the more powerful must be the incident forces which will divert the mental body from its original direction.

Recurring now to God's predestination and man's free will. If the events which surround each man's life are the inevitable results from the events which have been from the beginning of things, and if the congenital disposition of each man is the certain result of the lives of his ancestors, then both were known and foreordained from the beginning, and could not be otherwise, if God be indeed God, and if the laws of the universe are as the observation of mankind has shown them to be. Having therefore the two elements entering into the formation of man's choice given, the choice itself must be known. But this does not in the least do away with man's power of choice or free will, but on the contrary demands it. The reason why, man's circumstances and disposition being fully known, his choice may be predicted with certainty, is because his choosing is free to be acted upon by the forces concurrently acting upon it. Were the power of choice absent, or were it not free to be acted upon by circumstances and disposition, man's conduct could not be predicted in accordance with any laws that the human mind is familiar with. An infinite being may no doubt be credited with the power of arbitrarily looking into the future as a man would look into a page of a book to know its contents, without regard to anything that was before or after the given page, but we cannot appreciate or conceive of any such faculty. It is not here attempted to explain either nature or the Scriptures by assumptions of what may be beyond man's knowledge, but to explain both nature and the Scriptures in harmony with processes with which man is somewhat acquainted. Man being a part of nature and the Scriptures having been given for his enlightenment, the possibility of this is not an unwarrantable assumption. Therefore it is reiterated, that only by granting to man in theory what we note he is possessed of in fact, viz., free will, can we explain predestination in accordance with any laws known to man. The astronomer, knowing the characteristics of matter and knowing the circumstances of the planets, that is to say the things about them capable of influencing them, is able to predict with certainty where any given one will be at any given time. Why? Plainly because they are free to respond to the influences of their environment, are free to react upon it. Were the planets not free to move in entire obedience to their own constitution and the influence of their surroundings, foreknowledge of their positions would be an impossibility. So with regard to man, had he not perfect power of choice so that he could act in entire and exact obedience to the forces influencing his movements, prediction, foreknowledge and predestination would be an impossibility. But accept man's perfect free will and his ability to act in accordance with the forces of his environment, and his conduct, to one knowing both the play of forces within and without him, must be as certain as the position of the planet to the astronomer. There is then absolutely no contradiction between the doctrine of predestination and the doctrine of free will. The one is complementary to the other, and, so far as can be seen, the one could not exist without the other. There seems to be no escape from these conclusions.

CHAPTER XI

THE REVELATION OF LIFE

It is not improper from the standpoint of the scientific inquirer to ask what need there is of a revelation, because, according to the theory of evolution, natural agencies seem sufficient to produce the highest development which any species of life is capable of; and because investigation of the facts of life, so far as they are observable, seems to support the theory of evolution. For while many facts connected with living organisms are hard to explain in accordance with the doctrine of evolution, and some are now impossible of explanation, still the preponderance of evidence in its favor is so great that evolution in some form is the universally accepted belief of educated men at the present time. The honest inquirer may therefore without impropriety ask, from the standpoint of evolution, has not nature, within itself, the means of developing the highest grade of life without resort to a miraculous revelation from the realm of the supernatural?

THE REVELATION OF LIFE

Nor has the world been obliged to wait for the discovery of evolution, to be confronted by this same obtrusive question, concerning the need of revelation for the highest development of the human race. The student of history, and the observer of the course of events in his own day, has been puzzled or pleased (according to his convictions) to note the high attainments of certain men and nations without knowledge of or without belief in a supernatural revelation. The believer has endeavored to explain this state of facts in conformity with theology, while the unbeliever has regarded it as one of the impregnable strongholds of infidelity. Let us investigate the situation without bias.

What has been the progress and what have been the attainments of nations, on the one hand without the revelation of the Scriptures, and on the other with this revelation? History affords the best possible opportunities for studying this question both before and since the coming of Christ. Before Christ are the Greeks, Romans, Egyptians, Babylonians and other civilized races of antiquity on the one side and the Israelites on the other. Since the coming of Christ we have the so-called heathen nations on the one side and the Christian on the other. Let us first consider the nations of antiquity; they are not only first in order of time, but they exhibit the problem in simpler form. We find the Egyptians a highly civilized race at the very dawn of history. Whether we gain our ideas from the Scriptures or from the profane historians or from monuments or mummies or papyrus rolls, we gain the same idea of the ancient Egyptians. They were to a high degree intellectual and learned, they were far advanced in science and the arts of civilization; they were great, even judged by the standard of the abilities and attainments of the most favored people of the present century. Now we not only know the attainments of the ancient Egyptians in the arts of government and warfare, their knowledge of astronomical and mechanical principles, their literary ability and high social status, but we also have details of their religious beliefs. We are thus able to say with positiveness that they did not have the revelation of the Hebrew Scriptures, and that nevertheless they reached the highest intellectual level of the human race. Whatever nation ancient or modern we choose to use for the purpose of comparison, in intellectual ability and in garnered knowledge the Egyptian stands easily among the first. His ways and his works have com-

THE REVELATION OF LIFE 183

manded the admiration of the greatest intellects in all ages, even down to and including our own.

The Hebrew Scriptures reveal to us the Babylonians as a people high up in the scale of power and ability in war and civil government, standards of measurement of nations in all ages. Herodotus and other ancient historians described the Babylonians as not only excelling in military and civil affairs, but as the scientific nation of their times. In astronomy, architecture and the arts they stood in the forefront of the nations of their day. To the testimony of the historians is added that indisputable evidence literally unearthed by the researches of Layard, Rawlinson and their co-laborers, the evidence of the cylinders, bricks and monuments of ancient Assyria and Babylonia. The men of Assyria and Babylonia, as thus revealed to us, were mighty men indeed—mighty in intellect and science as well as mighty in valor. They were conquerors of ignorance as well as conquerors of nations.

Without stopping to further consider the attainments of their predecessors we come to the Greeks and Romans, practically amalgamated in the days of Christ. These wonderful races had gathered together and arranged for use all the treasures of the attainments of their predecessors. The stores of knowledge accumulated by Egyptians and Phoenicians, Assyrians, Babylonians and Persians, were all gathered together by the inquisitive Greek and the practical Roman, and made the means of still greater progress under their skillful manipulation. What have the men of the nineteenth century to boast of in the way of intellectual capacity over and above the ancient Greek and Roman? Absolutely nothing. No greater minds exist in our own day than existed in the Mediterranean Basin in the centuries before Christ. The generalship of Alexander, Hannibal and Caesar was the constant study and contemplation of the greatest captain of this century. Napoleon declared that the study of the doings of these men taught the art of war. From Caesar to Gustavus Adolphus nothing was added to the world's knowledge of this momentous art, the art of war. In so-called modern times only Gustavus, the great Frederick and Napoleon are deemed worthy of association with the three great captains of antiquity, Alexander, Hannibal and Caesar. Able generals there have been indeed, but only these three have pushed out the science of war-making beyond the boundaries fixed when Caesar fought his last battles. It is trite to remark what every schoolboy hears often, that in sculpture the Greeks produced models that artists have even until now been struggling to equal. In literature what genius of modern times has surpassed the masterpieces of the Golden Age of Greece and Rome? How readily can the products of the pen which can be placed alongside of these be counted. Even in this practical time Greek and Roman literature is regarded as a necessary element of a liberal education. In philosophy we note the same state of affairs; ancient Greeks brought forth master minds in this department, whose works are as well known to-day as they were in the first century of the Christian era. In science it is still the same; we have accumulated of late a vast store of knowledge of facts, but in intellectual grasp and powers of thought the philosophers of the present stand not a step in advance of their predecessors of ancient times. Turning from the intellectual to the moral side, the stern virtue of the ancient Greek and ancient Roman, before debauched with success and power, has been the admiration of mankind in all ages. It would be a rash controversialist who would dare assert that the ancient Spartan and the Roman of early days did not compare in moral virtues most favorably with the Italian, Spaniard and Frenchman of the Middle Ages; that Rome in the centuries preceding Christ did not in moral atmosphere compare favorably with the Rome of many centuries after Christ.

It will thus be seen that certain nations of antiquity who were without the revelation of the Hebrew Scriptures, who either had no knowledge of it or utterly disregarded it, nevertheless produced the very finest development of the human race, a development which in most particulars has never been surpassed, and regarded from a physical and mental standpoint probably never will be. These are indisputable facts, shutting one's eyes to them will not obliterate them.

Let us now turn to the Israelites, as the sole nation of antiquity favored with the revelation of the Scriptures. In the language of St. Paul, "What advantage then had the Jew?" Was the advantage one of physical or intellectual superiority, was it superiority in stern moral virtue, was it in knowledge of the arts and sciences, was it in social status, was it, in a word, in attainments in civilization as a nation and in the production of the highest examples of human individuals? The answer to these questions must certainly be,

THE REVELATION OF LIFE 187

no. Whether regarded as individuals or as a nation, it cannot in the light of history be contended that, as human beings, the Jews surpassed their neighbors who had not the revelation of the Scriptures. They had one great general in their very early days—David. David and Solomon were great statesmen, and the Israelitish rule seemed destined to rival in extent that of other nations of ancient times, the Egyptians, Assyrians, Babylonians and Persians. But judging either by the scriptural descriptions or by the known results, the Israelites did not afterwards produce warriors or statesmen of the first rank. In literature, indeed, nothing finer has ever been produced than that which comes from the Hebrew. But in architecture and all the arts and sciences of ancient times the Hebrews were only borrowers and adapters. Even their temple, the pride and glory of the nation, was due to the craft of the foreign Phoenician. The history of the Israelites, as shown in their own writings, gives no glimpse of originality in advancing civilization. As a people judged by their neighbors, they were great neither in the arts of peace nor war, save only in literature. As regards morality, *as a nation*, they seem to have been neither better nor worse than the nations surrounding them.

While idolatry was completely stamped out by the Babylonian captivity, the remedy applied by Ezra and Nehemiah and their successors, of exact and literal obedience to the injunctions of the law, in the end produced in the nation at large a narrow-minded, intolerant bigotry, so that it might almost be questioned whether the remedy was not worse than the disease. If regarded as a friend, a companion, an associate, a fellow-citizen, would not most men of to-day prefer the polished and liberal Greek or the broadminded, blunt and sturdy Roman to the Jew as exhibited either in sacred or profane history in the time of Christ?

But once again inquiring with St. Paul, and perhaps with an element of doubt in the inquiry, "What advantage then had the Jew?" the answer likewise is furnished by Paul. "Every way: first of all, that they were entrusted with the oracles of God." But this simply restates our inquiry in other terms. What was the advantage to the Jew of having entrusted to him the oracles of God or the revelation of the Hebrew Scriptures? It has been seen by a comparison of the attainments of the Jew, as a specimen of the human race, with the attainments of his contemporaries, that while he was in the same class with the

THE REVELATION OF LIFE

advanced nations of antiquity, he was not at the head of the class. Where then shall we look for the advantage to him of possessing the Scriptures? The advantage lay in the fact of the spiritualizing tendencies of the Hebrew revelation. If the object of the Hebrew revelation was to produce the finest exemplification of the human race, then history must pronounce the result a lamentable failure, because when Christ appeared upon the earth, the Greek and Roman peoples, judged by the standard of human perfection, as we would apply it even at this very day, had completely outstripped the "chosen people." And this is just exactly the contention of the unbeliever; and if the Christian accepts battle upon this issue as he has often done, he must suffer defeat, giving fresh zeal to the enemies of the Church, and burdening even the faithful with a needless weight of doubt, discouragement and anxiety. But if the object of the Hebrew revelation was not the development of the human race to ever higher states, but the preparation of individuals of that race for the reception of the life-giving impulse of the Spirit, the creation of that condition within the soul of man necessary for the birth of a new spiritual being having eternal life; if it rendered possible spiritual life to countless numbers of individuals under the old dispensation, and was a necessary part of the world's preparation for the comprehension and acceptance of Christianity, then the Hebrew revelation was an infinitely great and glorious success.

As we know there are two essentials for the birth of any new living organism: first a pre-existing living being, and second a suitable environment. If either of these essential prerequisites be wanting, no new living being will come into existence. As concerns the birth of new spiritual creatures, the first condition is supplied by the omnipresent Spirit, but the suitable environment is limited. As with all other life generation, the pre-existing living organism may be present, but the new living creature does not come into existence except within very narrow limits of suitable conditions. The seed and the egg are well-known examples; the condition of the pre-existing life has been fulfilled, but it is noticed that the bringing into existence of new living individuals depends upon very limited conditions of environment. Why should we not suppose that the essentials for the bringing into existence of new spiritual individuals should be similar; that the conditions permitting the creation of spiritual individuals are confined, as regards environment, within very narrow limits; and that while it might be possible for human beings by chance to bring themselves within these peculiarities of environment, the probabilities would be infinitely against it, unless the directions for the creation of the peculiar environment were revealed by the Power acquainted with its conditions? Let us make the supposition for the time, and see how this theory corresponds with the revelation of the Scriptures and the teachings of science.

The theory propounded takes it for granted that the conditions requisite for the effective action of the Spirit upon the human being, to beget a new spiritual being, is within the control of man himself, because the directions for the preparation were addressed to him. This supposition certainly corresponds with our knowledge of the creation of new living beings in the various kingdoms of life. Man is able to prevent the germination of life, and does do so in countless cases, and this notwithstanding one of the prerequisites of new life, the pre-existing life, is fulfilled. This he does by surrounding the pre-existing life with such conditions as render propagation impossible, or by surrounding the new living germ with such conditions as to destroy the budding life before it attains strength enough to resist adverse influences. He prevents the sprouting of seed so long as it suits his convenience to do so, by withholding from it the suitable conditions of temperature and moisture; he prevents the propagation of the germs of life by uncongenial degrees of heat and cold. He multiplies or prevents the increase of flocks and herds at pleasure; and in a thousand varying ways man is continually preparing or preventing a suitable environment for the propagation of new life. Nothing in biology, then, teaches us that there is anything improbable in the doctrine that man should control the preparation of an environment necessary for the propagation of spiritual beings. On the contrary there is much reason to suppose that this power, which man exercises with regard to all the lower forms of life, would continue to be his with regard to the higher.

Turning from science to the Scriptures, we find not only nothing against the supposition contended for, but its existence positively stated. The use of the Old Testament Scriptures and their success in attaining their object becomes at once clear if we regard their injunctions and directions as directed towards the creation of spiritual life and attainments, and not towards the development of human perfection. And this is the interpretation of the Old Testament in the New, for, says the writer of the Epistle to the Hebrews, "These all died in faith, not having received the promises, but having seen them and greeted them from afar, and having confessed that they were strangers and pilgrims on the earth. For they that say such things make but manifest that they are seeking after a country of their own. If indeed they had been mindful of that country from which they went out they would have had opportunity to return. But now they desire a better country, that is a heavenly: wherefore God is not ashamed of them to be called their God: for he hath prepared for them a city." Paul also states that the citizenship of the Christian is not of earth, but of heaven. The oracles of God, then, while incidentally giving to the Jews the best possible precepts for human happiness, were chiefly directed to preparing within them such a spiritual-mindedness as should fit them for obtaining citizenship in the realm of spiritual life. In the language of Paul, "What if some did not believe? Shall their unbelief make the faith of God without effect? God forbid." The influence of the oracles of God was in the direction of life, and they were sufficient for those who entrusted themselves to their direction. Moses and David and Isaiah were filled with a spirituality not exceeded even by the apostles.

But what is the nature of the environment which is thus a prerequisite of the generation of spiritual life, and which it was the office of the Old Testament revelation to declare? If it be not found in the highly developed human beings exemplified by the accomplished Egyptian, the polished Greek and the virtuous Roman, or the law-abiding Pharisee, of what does it consist and where shall we find an example of it? Is it external to the human being or internal? It is internal and may be summed up in one word—Christlikeness. Whether among Jews or Gentiles, whether in the mind of the believer or infidel, the word Christ brings before the mind a character and disposition which many words would not suffice to make clear. While Christ exhibited every human virtue, as mankind has regarded virtue, and possessed every desirable quality of mind and disposition which mankind has approved, there was in him something more and different. There is found in him in perfection those peculiarities of disposition which stamped Moses and Isaiah as being something different from the ordinary law-serving

THE REVELATION OF LIFE 195

Jew, something different from even the highest developed members of the ancient races of men. The nature of this environment is made most clear to us of to-day by calling it Christlikeness, but the nature of it was foreshadowed in the Old Testament from the first. There is a peculiar quality in even the very oldest Old Testament revelation, striking even a dull reader, rendering it something essentially different from the writings and teachings and sentiments of even the most lofty heathen writers. It was indeed calculated to make from Abraham a peculiar people; not, as we have seen, peculiar in greatness of conquest, in perfection of civil government, in progress in arts and sciences, in the graces of civilized life, nor yet in mere morality, because in all these things the Jews were equaled and sometimes surpassed by contemporaneous nations: but they became a peculiar people because there dwelt among them a peculiar spirituality. This word spirituality is used for lack of a better, it is used to denote certain qualities not developed nor indeed prized or appreciated by the most highly developed of the human races except as influenced by revelation. This spirituality, as exemplified by Moses and the prophets and David the king, showed its peculiarity in its possessor's reaching out towards something beyond his race and his time. Never was there stronger national feeling than that exhibited in the Jewish race, but nevertheless this spirituality showed itself by a longing for and a reaching out after a companionship not human, and a looking forward to (as the New Testament has it) "another country." It exhibited itself also in a peculiarity of thought and deed and a disposition running counter to mere human feeling and indeed human interest.

The law of Moses is regarded by many, if not most, as a mere compendium of ceremonies and injunctions of civil law; but an attentive reading disproves this conception. There is running through the whole law an undercurrent of principle as a thing distinct from the precept, and when we come to Deuteronomy its pages are fairly vital with a living, moving spirit of a higher life. The burden of the book is, thus do that ye may live.

The prophets, without in anywise going counter to the law, magnified the disposition, the state of mind of man, indicated indeed in the law, but almost overshadowed by it. The law was indeed a schoolmaster, the object plainly being to cultivate a disposition or frame of mind by exercise in those things which would naturally be the outcome of that disposition. But the prophets saw that some of the evidences of the thing were being mistaken for the thing itself; they therefore denounced in bitter terms the performance of the acts without the disposition intended to be cultivated by them. The law enjoined sacrifice as the outward manifestation of obedience, but the law-serving Jew offered the sacrifice in lieu of obedience, and brought down upon him the denunciations of the prophets who declared that mercy and not sacrifice was pleasing to God. Both law and prophets were giving directions for the cultivation of spirituality—Christlikeness.

But besides developing here and there a true spirituality among the Jews, the lawgiver, the psalmist and the prophet were instilling into the Jewish mind ideas of God and of spiritual things which should render Christ intelligible, and were putting upon record acts and experiences of mankind, and exhibiting states of mind and feeling, which were to furnish a storehouse of illustration, and become in the hands of Christ and his apostles a ready means of communication with the generation in which they lived. In reading the New Testament it seems impossible to conceive how its contents could have been known to the people in the days of Christ had there been no Jewish experience and no Hebrew revelation. The very vocabulary would have been lacking. The Jews of the days of Christ misinterpreted, in many fundamental matters, the law, the prophets, the psalms, but the possession of the knowledge of the oracles of God was there: in most instances misapplied, it is true, but none the less actually possessed for all that. The misinterpretation could be removed, but the lack of knowledge would have been fatal. The knowledge of the oracles of God possessed by the Jews was the common ground between them and Christ, which is necessary for all argument and conviction. The embodied religious experience of the Hebrew race enabled the disciples of Christ to apprehend and sufficiently comprehend the life and immortality which he first brought to light; and this same experience enabled the disciples of Christ to make plain to fellow human beings what otherwise had been a sealed book.

But it may be objected, this line of argument involves the idea that a given amount of cultivation, a given grade of intelligence is necessary in the human being in order to receive the spiritual meaning of the teachings of Christ. This may seem a somewhat startling proposition to some, for it rules out from the possibility of becoming Christian a large portion of the human race, past and present; but what are the facts? The Israelites were unable to receive the teachings of Moses at the time of the Exodus. The race was moved to flee out of Egypt by the terrible physical hardships of a grievous bondage; but in harmony with their low order of intellect and their selfish characters, they were no sooner a few days distant from the burdens of their servitude than savage-like they were conscious of nothing but present ills. And they seemed so utterly incapable of learning anything of the spiritual nature of God, so incapable of being controlled by anything that did not appeal to the grosser human-animal feelings, that the edict went forth that teaching them was a hopeless task, that the development of the nation demanded the destruction of those too old to learn and in their present state unfit to be trusted with the opportunities of the promised land. We know that the debased Israelites of Egypt perished rather than be taught. Under the Judges what a picture of apostasy! The Israelites seemed unable to distinguish the spiritual Jehovah from the idols of their neighbors. Even after the teachings of Samuel and David and the prophets of his day, the ordinary Israelite seemed to be totally unable to feel the spiritual power of his God. The sword and the pestilence, the invading army, the grasshopper and the drought were the only things that appealed to their gross feelings and slow intelligence. Driven by these tangible terrors out of idolatry, they for the most part could not see in their God anything higher than the arbitrary ruler. If this be not so, how are we to interpret the history of the Kings and the denunciation of the Prophets; and how are we to understand the part of the ordinary Jew in Christ's life and death?

Turning to our own times, what progress have missions made among the most degraded tribes? What has been accomplished for the Patagonians, the Bushmen, the Hottentots? And among higher races, has it not been observed that a certain grade of intelligence, a certain capacity of mind, a certain elevation of disposition has been necessary before, say, the Sermon on the Mount could be brought home to the hearer?

If we regard the negro race in the United States and study it closely, we find that the Christianity of the lowest class of negroes is something horribly grotesque. With many of the negroes in the Southern States

THE REVELATION OF LIFE

it is impossible to cause them to comprehend even the commonest principles of morality. Their passions, desires and actions are in many particulars much more easily compared with those of cattle than with those of the ordinary American citizen. It is no more possible to bring home the spiritual beauties of the Gospel to some of these beings than it would be to teach them the principles of spectrum analysis or the philosophy of Aristotle or Spencer. As the members of this race rise in the scale of intelligence and cultivation they are enabled to apprehend more and more of the truths of Christianity, until when a certain level is reached we find as noble and sincere Christians among them as are to be found anywhere in the world. To reiterate; the negro of the lowest class in the United States is a creature of such habits and disposition as not to be fit to be described in a book for general reading, and it seems impossible to cause this class to take hold of even the externals of Christianity; the gospels to him are a sealed book. Above these come the class who are able to comprehend and apprehend some of the broader principles of Christianity, and are particularly affected by ceremonial religion. They use some of the language of Christianity and seem to have imbibed in some degree its elevating principles; but what they have imbibed from Christianity is so mingled with superstition and misapprehension, and so degraded by minor vices, that the compound shocks the ordinary Christian when brought into close contact with it. Above this class are those who have reached a stage of intellectual capacity and disposition which enables them, although they may be able to neither read nor write, to accept and love and follow the precepts of Christ.

These indisputable facts indicate, or rather prove, that the human being, with all the mighty possibilities which his nature gives him, can only come into effectual contact with things spiritual when he has made a certain progress in things human. Christ said to Nicodemus, "If I told you earthly things and you believed not, how shall you believe if I tell you heavenly things?" Some capacity for the apprehension of earthly things, a certain human capacity is a prerequisite for the attainment of the knowledge of heavenly things. We learn from the Scriptures that the Church was founded among the Jews, a people of high intellectual powers, cultivated to a high degree, and learned in all the accumulated knowledge of the age and in the peculiar experiences of the Jewish race. It extended in apostolic times to the boundaries of the Roman Empire. Certainly these things were not accidental. In the fullness of time Christ came. He came when the human race had arrived at a stage of sufficient cultivation to receive him. All writers on the life of Christ or the apostles agree in regarding the Greek and Roman civilization as a preparation for the coming of Christ. They might go further and say that without it, humanly speaking, the propagation of the Christian religion could not have been effected. That the Church should have been founded and progressed as it did, only amidst the highly cultivated races, and that it has been confined ever since to the same class of men, seems inexplicable on any other supposition than that a certain level of intellectual capacity must be reached, and that a certain disposition of mind must be attained—in other words, that a certain amount of cultivation must exist in the human being before it is prepared to receive intelligence of spiritual things, and, acting in accordance with this intelligence, obtain spiritual life.

But leaving the Old Testament revelation and its effects, let us note the progress and attainments of the human race without and with the New Testament revelation. It may be said without fear of contradiction that the Christian nations have far outstripped the heathen nations in the race of civilization. But the highly civilized state of the Christian nations may prove either one of two things, either that high culture and great attainments in the arts of civilization follow Christianity or that Christianity follows civilization. As in many another similar case, the truth probably lies between, and the thing proven is that Christianity and the development of the civilization of the human race each conduces to the other.

Christianity found man at his highest independent development. This development of man as a preparation for the growth of the spiritual kingdom was necessary, but it was accomplished by forces existing in the human race and in its so-called natural surroundings. That the ordinary forces of development were sufficient is proved by the progress made by the nations without revelation. Revelation was added to pre-existing influences not because higher species of human beings were required, but because a new kind of being was required; and the visible and notorious effect produced by Christianity upon the human race is the result of the influence of this new and superior upon an old and inferior order of beings. The so-called humanizing of mankind since Christ is just the reverse: it is a spiritualizing. If we wish to find the pure human characteristics of mankind we must search for them among those nations where revelation has not existed and where the Christians have not come in contact with them. The closest study of peoples unconnected with the Hebrews of ancient days and the Christians of modern times fails to show what is now comprehended under the term " humane." The altruistic sentiments which have developed in the Christian nations, the sentiment of the brotherhood of the human race, the great altruistic principle of Christ, " Do unto others as ye would that others should do unto you," the spirit of charity which finds its expression in the voluntary care of the sick, the poor, the helpless and the oppressed—in a word, all the so-called humanitarian principles of the present age, were not found in the nations either before or since Christ, outside the range of the influence of revelation; and inside this range all these principles are found reduced to a minimum where the true spiritual Christianity has waned. It is this spiritualization of the human race that constitutes the debt of the world to Christianity. Material prosperity, intellectual enlightenment have undoubtedly been incidents of the Christian life in the midst of the peoples, but it is waste of time to dispute with the infidel whether these incidental results can be traced to Christianity or no. It is the ennobled disposition of Christian civilization that creates the incalculable obligation of Christian civilization to Christianity.

That this ennobled disposition is possessed by myriads of men who not only do not follow but with a greater or less activity oppose the Christian faith, is no argument against the claims of Christianity. On the contrary, when rightly considered it affords valuable support. If the true Christians are all members of a spiritual kingdom, higher in perceptions and corresponding with a broader environment and possessing higher powers than mere human beings, then we should expect that little by little they would effect changes in the inferior race with which they are brought into such constant and intimate relations. Every one perceives the marvellous effect which man has produced upon certain lower orders of living creatures. Who supposes for one moment that the "almost human" dog or horse would be in certain characteristics so much like their masters had they

THE REVELATION OF LIFE

not been in contact with them? Whence have the collies and the setters their now inborn characteristics of herding and hunting? Without dispute from the influence through generation after generation of man. All are aware that the highly improved races of cattle and sheep and domesticated animals in general have arrived at their present highly improved condition, and have become possessed of many of their characteristics, through contact with the human race. Why then should not the members of the spiritual kingdom, acting through countless generations upon the human race, have developed in it certain characteristics of their own, which the human race left to itself would have had neither the power nor the inclination to develop? If the principles of the members of the spiritual race are those enunciated in the New Testament, and if every person born into the kingdom is under biological laws bound to possess the characteristics of his race, then the members of the kingdom must in each succeeding generation possess the same characteristics, and some of these unvarying characteristics will become more and more impressed upon the inferior race of human beings until they become hereditary. Therefore there is nothing strange in finding highly developed Christian or spiritual traits in human beings who reject Christ. They have inherited these qualities, and can only rid themselves of them by the same sort of process as they may rid themselves of an inherited strong physical constitution. As in other cases of living beings, the inferior race sooner or later reverts to its original condition when removed from environing influences which have produced special traits. So it is discovered that men and races, once having many Christian characteristics, lose these characteristics when removed from the Christianizing influences. It is likewise learned from history and observation that when Christianity degenerates into mere morality and formalism, when, in other words, the spiritual life as distinct from some of its manifestations disappears, the Christian virtues do not long remain behind. It is plain therefore that were the true spiritual beings to disappear from the earth, the so-called humanizing tendencies of the human race would speedily follow.

Those who by virtue of their acquired spiritual traits and powers criticise some of the doings and sayings of the Old Testament people as inhuman, could they view these inhuman matters from the standpoint of the highest unassisted human development, would doubtless be astonished to find their inhumanity utterly disappear. It is a most common characteristic of the human mind to read previous events and expressions in the light of subsequent ones, and to read into the past the experience of the present. And thus it happens that cultivated men of to-day, possessed of the inherited traits acquired from Christianity through generations, erroneously judge the men of the past, in whom spiritual forces had not yet developed such well-marked spiritual traits as those exhibited in themselves. Mistaking their own induced spirituality for humanity, while contemplating themselves; and contrariwise confounding human passions with spiritual influences, when viewing the men of old; and ignoring a fundamental tenet of evolution, that it is prodigal in its use of time, they express themselves as much shocked that spiritual forces did not produce upon the human race as much effect in one generation as they have in a hundred.

If the history of God's dealings with mankind, as exhibited in the Scriptures, be viewed in the same manner as the history of the working of natural forces, as revealed in the book of nature, it will be found that the method evinced is the same in both. That is to say, certain forces are brought to bear upon living beings, and not at once, but by imperceptible increments, bring about results. If growth in nature does not move in leaps, why should we expect a different rule when regarding the effect of spiritual forces upon the human race? Let it be granted that Abraham, Jacob, David and other Old Testament saints exhibited traits which, judged by the highest standards of to-day, shock the moral sensibilities, what are we to infer? That the God of the Hebrew differs from the God of the Christian, or that the principles of the Old Testament oppose those of the New? By no means. As in all other cases, we infer that the forces at work changed the species acted upon by slow degrees. Moreover, as we are compelled to measure movement, when it is slow, not by distant but by nearby objects, so to gain correct information concerning Old Testament revelation and its influence upon the Hebrews we must compare the acts and principles of the people of Israel with those of surrounding nations. By so doing we discover that in spiritual qualities, in "humanity," as we in these days term it, the people of Israel were nearer the Christian nations of the present day than they were to their most civilized contemporaries. That the men

THE REVELATION OF LIFE

of Israel fell far below the men of the nineteenth Christian century, when measured by the pure standards of the Scriptures, which have become the standards of civilization, is what we should expect from the laws of evolution to find.

But while for that communion of the Spirit with the human life which is necessary for the generation of new spiritual beings, human life must reach a certain high level of development, and while for this development the ordinary evolutionary forces seem to be sufficient, nevertheless the needed preparation demands certain elements not produced by the ordinary forces of nature. The very highest examples of intellectual and moral manhood have remained untouched by the spirit life of Christianity both in ancient and modern times. And these examples may have exhibited in themselves, along with these high human traits, so many of the characteristics of spirituality that it is sometimes not a little difficult to perceive the one thing which they yet lack. The forces of evolution, natural selection, heredity and the rest serve to secure an ever-increasing prominence of the communicated spiritual traits of mankind, so far as these traits may be possessed by the inferior human race. Just as certain physical characteristics of good circulation, or sound tissue, which are the direct results of that conduct which is the natural concomitant of certain mental and moral qualities, may be transmitted to progeny, which nevertheless may not exhibit, in any marked degree, the mental and moral qualities which originally produced them; so certain qualities of body and mind, produced by spiritual influences of Christianity, may be transmitted to progeny, who nevertheless never accept the revelation of Christ nor obtain the life to which it points. It was no doubt a cause of great astonishment to the young man who not only recounted but exhibited in his very person his manifold virtues to Christ, to be told by him that he yet lacked something to make possible his entrance into the kingdom of heaven. Much more, probably, did it astonish the ordinary beholder. But there was wanting in his character some necessary element to enable him to receive the vital spark of spiritual life; and lacking this one necessary element, for the purpose of receiving the new life, he lacked all. Thus many lack much and all lack something without the teaching of revelation. The knowledge of the lacking elements of preparation and the methods of producing them are furnished by revelation. Therefore while each succeeding generation exhibits the world more and more fitted for the reception of Christianity and its spiritual life, each generation needs as much as the first the divine revelation. This is the plain declaration of the Scriptures, for it says there can be no salvation except through faith in Christ, and how shall they believe of whom they have not heard, and how shall they hear unless they are preached unto? Each man as an individual needs to be told of Christ and his revelation to prepare him for the reception of the life eternal.

CHAPTER XII

THE NECESSITY OF FAITH

It may now perhaps be easier to understand why belief is and must be the keystone of the arch supporting the Gospel plan for securing eternal life. For if a revelation be necessary to bring to light the existence of a new kingdom of life and to teach the means necessary to employ in order to gain entrance into it, then a belief in the revelation becomes just as necessary.

Belief is the mainspring of all effective human action. No undertaking is begun except there is some belief that it may be accomplished; doubt concerning accomplishment goes a long way towards securing defeat. That confidence concerning the result goes far towards bringing it about is universally acknowledged. Alexander would never have conquered Persia without his belief that none could resist his power. Much is said concerning Napoleon's belief in his guiding star, but it was Napoleon's belief in his own ability, his profound confidence in himself which enabled him to become the dictator of Europe. The never-failing source of endurance and aggressiveness in the American Revolution was the unwavering belief of Washington in the eventual success of the colonists. Washington was a good general and a good statesman, but what placed him in the undisputed first place among the great men of the Revolutionary epoch was the steadfastness of his belief. A little variableness on his part would upon more than one occasion have wrecked the cause of the Colonies. Rarely has a cause so completely depended upon one man as did that of the Free States depend upon Lincoln. When the war of the rebellion had become a thing of the past and the actors in it could be viewed from such a distance as to measure their heights, Lincoln was seen to tower alone, although he was surrounded by many men mighty in intellect and executive ability. In the days between the inauguration and the firing upon Fort Sumter, Mr. Lincoln alone and single-handed saved the Union, because he alone had no doubts. The brilliant generals, statesmen and orators, who were the leaders in the Republican party, were one and all seized with faintness, seemingly aghast at the logical outcome of the labor of their lives. Lincoln alone was firm in the faith.

He then arose above all and remained above all. He believed not indeed that God was upon his side, but that he was upon God's side, and that there could be but one outcome; and his success was measured by his belief. Who does not know what belief accomplishes in war? The commander's confidence in his troops, and the soldiers' belief in the ability of the commander are such powerful factors as to counterbalance almost any numerical advantages. When, for instance, at the battle of Ruspina, Caesar found himself with ten thousand men in the midst of an open plain, attacked by sixty thousand men, one might suppose extermination inevitable. Many of his army were raw recruits; they knew of the extermination of Curio's army not long before, and betrayed by their looks their anxiety for the outcome of the fight. Nor were their fears unfounded, for the flanks of the little army could not be protected, and nothing could prevent its being outflanked and attacked in front and rear. The slightest knowledge of military affairs leads one to know that the one peculiarly fatal thing in war is the enemy in the rear, but Caesar believed in himself and his men believed in him. Numbers therefore did not avail the enemy, and victory once again rested with the

THE NECESSITY OF FAITH

legions of Caesar. No one can suppose that this would have been the result had doubt reigned in the place of confidence. Military history is full of examples of the power of belief.

Men leave the sinking ship for the boat which comes to the rescue because they believe that they will be lost if they remain, and that they will be saved if they take to the boat. Belief then in this case is just as necessary for their salvation as is the boat; a failure to believe either that the ship is sinking or that the boat will convey them to safety will be fatal to life. When one is warned by a friend that the house is on fire he is indeed saved by the friend, but just as much by belief, because had he not believed in the warning he would have remained and been lost. What distinguished Columbus from his contemporaries was not superior knowledge, but belief. The theory that the world was round was not new with Columbus; he was not the discoverer of the idea, he simply believed in it. Had he not believed in the rotundity of the earth he would not have entered upon his voyage; had he not believed in the truthfulness of the magnetic needle, despite its variation, he would have abandoned his voyage. Thus literally by his belief he discovered the New World.

Nor need belief be strong like Alexander's, Caesar's or Lincoln's to effect success: though it be only as a grain of mustard seed it may be sufficient. It may indeed be smaller than the mustard seed, invisible to beholders, and yet answer. The man who deserts the steady ship which gives no indication to his inexperienced eye of danger may scarcely believe the word of the sailor that she is sinking; again, the tossing boat alongside seems to him almost certain to be swamped, nay, he may be thoroughly convinced, so far as he is conscious of an opinion, that the boat will never convey him to safety. And yet, though he may declare that he expects to be drowned, he must just a little believe that there is a shadow of a chance for safety or he would stay where he is. The terrified inmate of a burning building looks out from the dizzy height to the pavement below, notes the ladder swaying under the weight of the climber, and says to himself he will never be able to make the descent, but he tries nevertheless because he believes just a little. Doubtless many a soldier in the little army on the plain of Ruspina thought the chance more than desperate, but still Caesar had found a way of escape from many a bad place before, and it might be that even now, desperate as the

THE NECESSITY OF FAITH 219

situation seemed, he would save them. Men toil for years if belief in an ultimate success holds out, but the man absolutely discouraged sinks into inactivity. It seems impossible to conceive of any human action which is not the result of some degree of belief. It may be weak, so weak as to seem unbelief, and yet where there is action it must be present.

Unbelief is fatal to success, to safety, and ofttimes to life, because it causes the neglect of the means to secure or preserve them. "He who doubts is damned" is as true as it is trite. A man would not even eat if he did not believe that food would stay hunger, nor drink unless he believed that water would quench thirst. The Bible thus teaches no strange doctrine when it says that belief is essential to salvation, but when examined it is found to be one which embodies the experience of mankind.

But believing is important only because it leads to doing: it is because if we do not believe we will not act, and if we do not act we shall not accomplish, that we must believe or fail. It is this belief which leads to action that constitutes faith. For if belief does not lead to action it is like the seed which never sprouts—it promises results but yields none. "Faith without works is dead." There is no efficiency in mere belief.

Faith is an action-compelling force. Like other forces it is invisible, intangible, and is only known by its effects; if it produces effects we know it exists, it is present; if it does not, we cannot know it does exist or is present. That mere belief has no saving efficiency is also shown by the fact that the same belief, sincere and well-founded, may be the actual salvation of one man and entirely fail to save another. The captain who by his inexcusable negligence has run his vessel upon the rocks, and his passengers may have exactly the same belief that the ship is doomed, that to remain is death, that an efficient way of escape is provided by the line from the shore. Yet this identical belief saves the passenger, because he wishes to escape, and may not save the captain because he has no desire to survive the consequences of his fatal neglect. Belief is indeed necessary for salvation, but does not insure it. Only when it is alive, when it is a force, when it causes action, is it of any avail.

Not even when faith is an active force is it always effective to produce salvation. Just as different physical forces neutralize and modify each other's tendencies, so different beliefs neutralize and modify each other's effects. One may have a lively belief in

Christ and his teachings which prompts him to pursue the way which he is fully persuaded leads to a better life. Now with this belief say there also exist such others as that there is yet a sufficiency of time to attend to these matters; that it would now be inconvenient and unnecessary to make a change; that other interests are, for the present only, more important. Any or all of these other beliefs may so modify the effects of the first that no efficient action will ever result. If such a one be saved he will have been saved by means of his belief, but he may be lost in spite of it.

The tendencies of belief may also be resisted by other forces in the mind. One may believe in Christ and feel powerfully impelled to follow him, but resisting this impulse of faith may be impulses of appetite and passion; love of wealth or honor or advantage, hatred, malice, envy, may one or all be impelling those whom they possess in directions which will never lead to the way of life. If belief in Christ co-exist with these antagonistic forces, it may be long, it may be never, before it overcomes them. So belief may fail to save because it is mere belief, and therefore dead, or because it is hindered or overcome by other antagonistic beliefs and passions. Believing something, then, resolves itself practically into doing something.

If belief be considered as a force, causing action, then from analogy we should suppose that different kinds of belief would produce different kinds and amounts of action, and we should not be surprised to find it asserted that a belief in Christ as a good man will not serve as a substitute for the belief in Christ as the Son of God, as a means of obtaining eternal life. The fire upon the hearth and the ticking of the clock above it both cause motion in the surrounding air; but how essentially different are the final results. The fire drawing the surrounding air to itself propels it through the chimney into the limitless regions of the atmosphere, and its field of activity thenceforth is boundless. The ticking of the clock, however, merely causes the particles of air to vibrate to and fro within the four walls which contain it. The ticking clock, though it should keep the imprisoned air in motion for a thousand years, would never open to it the infinite possibilities of the outside world. The explosion of dynamite will agitate the air for miles around, but it is nothing but agitation; the particles of air vibrate to and fro for a time, but eventually come to rest in the same place which they occupied when their movement began; but the rays of the sun start the air upon a journey, the length of which no man can estimate. So beliefs may either merely agitate or they may propel. In the one case the individual may be driven to great activity in a limited sphere, but remain in the end what and where he was in the beginning. In the other case he may be drawn or forced out of his old environments, become subjected to new and different forces, and in the end become an entirely new and different being. It must be borne in mind that success demands not merely that we do, but also do enough. It may well be that one belief might lead the holder of it to stop short of his journey's end, to his destruction, while another belief would urge him on to complete the journey before he rested and secure safety. Belief in its own abilities may enable a garrison to repel the first assaults, belief in their own resources and in that of their leaders may hold them still longer to their work, but when these are exhausted it may be necessary to add belief in sure and timely relief from without to enable them to endure to the end and be saved. The truth is indeed mighty, and the mere propounding of it has a powerful influence for good upon the hearers of it. We are not surprised, therefore, to find the teachings of Confucius, of Socrates, of Plato, of Christ, working wonders upon the characters of men, though unaccompanied by any belief in the divinity of their origin. But in the very nature of things we should suppose that a belief in Christ as God omniscient, omnipresent, sympathizing, considering, protecting his people, would more powerfully influence the holders of it than would the belief in Christ as a human teacher of even matchless worth.

Many expressions in the Bible make faith synonymous with life, and our ordinary use of the word follows the scriptural example. In a sense this is correct, because without belief in the means necessary to produce it there can be no life. We make a similar use of language in speaking about the life of the body and some of its necessary concomitants. For example, we speak of shedding a man's blood as equivalent to killing him or taking his life; we talk of requiring his blood in expiation of some injury, meaning thereby requiring his life; we speak of his blood being upon his own head, meaning that he is responsible for his own death; we say, too, there is no breath in him, meaning no life, and so on. In other words, we put for life something without which it cannot exist. In this way it is proper to use faith and life interchangeably, and it is done constantly both in

THE NECESSITY OF FAITH 225

the Bible and in common speech, meaning only that faith is a necessary concomitant of life. Faith may be used synonymously with life because faith leads to the sole source of life. The life-giving impulses are near at hand and on every hand, but man must put himself in contact with them or life will never be his. Faith leads him to do this, and thus it is that "he that believeth hath life and he that believeth not hath not life."

Faith involves obedience and obedience involves conformity to law—conformity to the forces which act upon us and around us. Belief does not involve comprehension, scarcely even expectation; this *do* and thou shalt be saved, is the injunction and the promise. Believing is said to be a state of mind and beyond our control, and therefore a conditioning of salvation on belief is unjust. Very well, but obedience is within our control and is all that is required. Many entirely miss the scriptural conception of faith by confounding it with understanding or comprehension. If man's inheritance of eternal life depended upon his understanding the forces involved in it his case would indeed be hopeless. Christ endeavored to show this to Nicodemus, when he likened the power of the Spirit to the wind. The effects of the wind were easily seen and comprehended, but true is it that man neither knows whence it cometh nor whither it goeth, or why it either comes or goes. Modern science has indeed explained much that is mysterious concerning the winds, but after all little is known concerning the laws which control the movements of the atmosphere. Yet something is known, and that something is enough; for the mills grind and the ships sail and men regulate many of the affairs of daily life by taking advantage of the force of the wind and its varied effects. The rude fisherman uses the force of the wind with not the slightest comprehension of whys and wherefores; enough for him that the winds blow and the sails draw; the physical geographer with all his knowledge of currents and cyclones might get no more benefit from it. So long as the sailor properly adjusts his sails to the breeze and takes advantage of its power he is as well off as though he understood all the laws of mechanics. To take advantage of the power of the wind naught is required except to note its power and to use proper means to place one's self within the influence of it. Comprehension of the nature of the power is not at all necessary.

That faith does not involve comprehension

THE NECESSITY OF FAITH 227

is exemplified continually in the case of the student. The text-book is placed within his hands: he finds stated within it many strange propositions, many a proposition which in the light of his present experience seems so utterly improbable as scarcely to be believed and not at all to be comprehended. Is it a work on chemistry, then he may find the statement meeting his eye that if two colored, solid, insoluble, inodorous substances be united together they will produce a colorless, foul-smelling, liquid substance; and directions are given for uniting sulphur and carbon to produce bisulphide of carbon. He performs the experiment and lo! the result, strange though it seems, is produced. Now in this case faith did not involve comprehension, and involved only so much belief in the possibility of the result as to induce him to try the experiment. He is further told in the same book that an inflammable gas (hydrogen) unites with another gas (oxygen) in which even watch-springs burn like tinder, to form water, which is to his mind the very opposite of fire. He tries the experiment and once more the statement is true. Or leaving the student of science and turning to agriculture, the field has as many surprises as the laboratory. Why should stirring the earth counteract the effect of drought? To this day scientific men do not agree in their explanations, but the farmer knows the advantage of well-tilled ground. The novice need not understand, nor is he expected to understand, nor is it needful that he should understand, but if he would succeed he must till. It is hard to divest ourselves of our experience, but why should not seeds grow as well on top of the ground as underneath it; and if underneath it, why must they be at one depth rather than another? What farmer understands these things, and yet he lives and the world lives by faith in the principles concerned, and faith, as is seen, necessarily involves obedience. The farmer may in his mind be never so well convinced that it is unnecessary to till the ground so long as in point of fact he does till it, and his belief in the efficacy of tillage will avail him naught provided his plough and hoe are idle.

So it is in regard to spiritual matters; so long as the power is recognized, and so long as we have information enough to utilize the power, no more is required, and but little more is given. It is in nowise necessary that we should understand or comprehend the spiritual life, any more than we should understand the physical life or the workings of physical forces. Nor is it necessary that we should understand how certain means at our disposal bring eternal life, any more than it is necessary for us to understand how means at our disposal unlock the forces of nature. What is necessary is that we should first recognize the object to be obtained and then use the means which we are told will secure it. Not comprehension but obedience is the necessary thing. Failure is only to be excused by the impossibility of obedience; but since the directions which we are to obey are possible to be performed by all, since the means to be used are within the reach of all, and since the methods of using them are within the comprehension of all, there can be no excuse. Where the good to be gained is very great, and the means recommended are to be had as by raising the hand, nothing save folly unspeakable can justify the refusal to make trial.

But what guarantee attaches to the directions of the Scripture? The same guarantee which attaches to the directions by which man governs his ordinary life. Infinite forces, the nature of which are but little or not at all understood, are in operation all about him; he believes in their existence because he sees their effects, and he must regulate his conduct so as to move in harmony with them at his peril. The wind is not the only incomprehensible force of which he sees the effects and of which he takes advantage to add to his powers to make pleasant his life and to prolong it. Heat and light and sound and the force of gravity, the mysterious vital forces of the animal and vegetable world touch his life at every point; and these and other agencies he must consider and act upon continually. Consciously or unconsciously he must place himself in harmony with the ever-active forces about him, or he ceases to live and that quickly.

CHAPTER XIII

THE MYSTERY OF REVELATION

But it may be objected that the revelation of a real spirit life distinct from the ordinary human life is full of mystery, that it takes us out of the regions of fact and into the realms of fancy. It is no argument against a thing that imagination has been called in to assist in the building of it. Without the scientific use of the imagination science makes little progress. The poet and philosopher are near akin, the difference being that the latter must submit his fancy to the test of harmony with fact. The very words "soul," "ghost" and "spirit" are inseparably connected with the mysterious, as well they may be. The material for forming hypotheses concerning what these words denote is scanty, and facts for verification are few indeed. We do not, however, leave mystery behind when, leaving the products of imagination and theory, we enter upon the so-called solid ground of fact. The mysterious is not always wonderful, any more than the incomprehensible is always strange.

It is much urged against religion that it deals so largely in mystery. Its mysteriousness is not to be denied. "Great is the mystery of godliness," is the Scriptures' own declaration. But so far from its being an argument against religion, it is just the reverse. The realm of science is crowded with mystery, and its so-called knowledge is built as much upon unverifiable hypotheses as is religion. The very "facts" which the skeptic is so fond of referring to are as thoroughly wrapt in mystery as ever any declaration in the Scriptures concerning the unseen universe. Even those who resort to materialism as the only sure foundation rest themselves upon mysteries as profound as anything in the Apocalypse. What after all does man know of that which he calls matter, which seems so solid and substantial to build upon? Whence came it? There is nothing in religion which could any more baffle our attempts at comprehension than the mere existence of matter. It is no more difficult to believe in the eternity of God than the eternity of matter. Leaving matter and turning to less tangible things in nature, we find mystery still. Sound is vibration, science now tells us, communicated through some appropriate medium, be it air or water or metal or what not. But we know of sound only by hearing, which science once again tells us is the communication of these vibrations through the air or other medium to the auditory nerve and thence to the brain. But why this produces within us the sensation we call hearing, who can tell? What impenetrable mystery surrounds what we know as the " correlation of forces "—the conversion of heat into electricity, electricity into sound, sound again into heat. We explain this possibility of transforming these various forces, the one into the other, by calling them all modes of motion. This involves our filling by means of our imagination the universe with vibrating matter. But who upon contemplating the fact that the etherial vibration called light, which now is entering his eye, left its birthplace on some distant star when the human race still was young, does not feel the pressure of mystery upon him? But whether we note the germinating seed, the growing plant, the budding flower, the moving wind, the floating cloud, the forming crystal, the world organic or inorganic, life or death, we find the visible world teeming with the marvellous and mysterious on every hand. Science is pushing out the boundaries of knowledge in every direction, but knowledge everywhere ends in profound and impenetrable mystery.

Therefore that mystery surrounds religion and that its known principles pushed far enough out lead to insoluble enigmas, and that its principles, seemingly thoroughly verified in one field, appear upon projection to conflict with equally well-verified principles in other fields, and that at last we must exclaim with the Psalmist, "Who by searching can find out God?" but makes the Word of God in thorough harmony with his works. To use the language of science, the mystery of godliness and the mystery of nature are but different manifestations of the same thing. As well may the chemist, with the final inexplicability of the atomic theory on his hands, taunt the biologist with the "missing link"; as well may the physicist, with the insoluble enigma of a final explanation of the correlation of forces ever present with him, make sport of the mathematician who works upon the hypothesis that a sufficient number of straight lines can make a curved one; as that a true philosopher should ask the Christian that he should exhibit something to him without mystery.

The man of science regards the infinite universe about him as an order of things in the course of explanation. He does not allow himself to become oppressed by the infinity of the unknown, nor does he hesitate to seek for knowledge in one direction because that which he has learned in another still lacks completeness. The true philosopher does not hesitate to grasp and use that which is within reach because of that which is still beyond it. The same course should be pursued towards religion. Mystery in religion should not be regarded as a bar while it is not so regarded in science.

Turning from those who object to the religion of the Scriptures because it abounds in the mysterious, we find another class whose objections are the very reverse—those who admit the existence of God, but claim that he is an impenetrable mystery. They declare that science points to the Infinite Unknown and they do not choose to combat the existence of God. They claim, however, that He must be infinite, unconditioned, incapable of definition, revelation or comprehension. So far from objecting to the mysterious, the agnostic revels in it. The agnostic science of the present day has been of inestimable advantage to Christianity. It is rapidly driving out of existence objections to religion on account of its mystery. In the opinion of one of the apostles of evolution, " The mystery, which all religions recognize, turns out to be a far more transcendent mystery than any of them suspect—not a relative but an absolute mystery." Of ultimate scientific ideas his declaration is that they "are all representative of realities that cannot be comprehended." Now if these ideas sown by men of science take root among the people—and they certainly seem to be taking root—there will soon be left no place for those who will accept none of what they cannot completely understand, for it will be common knowledge that we can completely understand nothing.

But if the agnostic insists that God is unknowable, he as strenuously insists on his existence. Herbert Spencer says: "Thus the consciousness of an inscrutable power manifested to us through all phenomena has been growing ever clearer, and must eventually be freed from all its imperfections. The certainty that on the one hand such a power exists, while on the other hand its nature transcends intuition and is beyond imagination, is the certainty towards which intelligence has from the first been progressing. To this conclusion science inevitably arrives as it reaches its confines; while to this conclusion religion is irresistibly driven by criticism. And satisfying as it does the demands of the most rigorous logic at the same time that it gives the religious sentiment the widest possible sphere of action, it is the conclusion we are bound to accept without reserve or qualification." These quotations from Mr. Spencer express to a hair's breadth the doctrine of the Scriptures as to the infinity of God and the utter inability of the human intellect to comprehend him. Thus far the Christian may seemingly travel the same road with the modern agnostic, and willingly acknowledge the service rendered by the lusty blows delivered right and left amid the forces of "science falsely so-called." He cannot, however, understand the position of the agnostic when he denies the possibility of God's making a revelation to man concerning the spiritual as distinguished from the natural world. This last position of the agnostic seems to be in complete contradiction to his own generalizations concerning ultimate scientific and religious ideas, and man's inability to comprehend the ultimate essence of things, either scientific or religious. If it be admitted that all the phenomena of nature are but the manifestations of an unknown reality behind them which cannot be comprehended, it must also be admitted that a comprehension of these phenomena or appearances as manifestations of the unknown reality suffices to enable man to so order his conduct, as to harmonize with the unknown as manifested, and thereby to obtain life and happiness. It is in nowise necessary for man to comprehend the infinite power or cause which lies behind things, as they appear to him, and forces, as they act upon him and about him. He is well enough acquainted with nature when he becomes acquainted with nature as manifested to him. He is not concerned with the ultimate essence of electricity; it suffices him to be acquainted with the manner in which the ultimate essence manifests itself to him. Philosophically considered, of the ultimate essence of things natural, man can know nothing, since the finite cannot comprehend the infinite; but he comprehends that portion of the infinite with which, so to speak, he comes in contact, and with the rest he is not concerned. It may most truly be said that no person really knows any other person; all that one person knows of another is the manifestations of that other. The real person behind the outward manifestations of conduct is as utterly beyond our reach as that infinite power of which natural phenomena are the manifestations. And yet knowing the phenomena, so to speak, of a person—knowing, in other words, the conduct of the person, we know enough for all the practical purposes of life. Since then all our knowledge of things natural is knowledge of the manifestations of those things to us, and since such knowledge seems to be all that is necessary for life and happiness, why should it be asserted that, albeit we cannot comprehend God, he cannot manifest himself to us; and that man, knowing these manifestations of him, should not know God just as truly as he knows a friend or any other thing in nature?

The infinite power has manifested itself to human intelligence through the phenomena of nature. What scientific warrant is there for asserting that this power which is infinite should not manifest itself to human intelligence by words as well as works? Why should it not have manifested itself to the consciousness of man without the intervention of known natural phenomena, as well as through them? What is there against the inherent probability of the infinite power manifesting itself to the human race through the best-adapted medium, the human organization?

With the agnostic, the Christian makes no attempt to define or to comprehend his infinite God; differing from the agnostic, he sees nothing either impossible or improbable in

God's revealing to man such a finite manifestation of himself as shall enable man to act in conformity with the laws of his universe, natural or supernatural, visible or unseen. The Christian admits, with the agnostic, that unaided by supernatural revelation he can know only of the natural; but differing from the agnostic, he sees no reason why the infinite power behind nature should not make a revelation to beings within the kingdom of nature, of things beyond the kingdom of nature. And supposing the revelation to be made to man of things pertaining to a realm outside of nature, he would think it not only probable but necessary that intelligence of things supernatural should be rendered into terms natural. Granting that there is a realm outside of nature, and that a revelation of it needed to be made to man, then it must needs be translated into human forms to be comprehended by human beings: in other words, the revelation of God to man, the revelation of things spiritual to beings human, must be anthropomorphological. To recapitulate: since we know nothing of the infinite power behind nature except the manifestations of that power, and since there is no scientific warrant for limiting the manifestations of that power to natural phenomena, and since intelligence to be communicated to human beings must be translated into forms of human thought, and since the most perfect medium of revelation to mankind must be man, the scriptural revelation, and particularly the revelation of God through Christ, is not only not impossible, it is not even improbable; and furthermore, the anthropomorphological character of the religion of the Scriptures, which causes so much unhappiness to many, is an inherent necessity of any revelation to human intelligence.

Let us examine this mystery of the revelation concerning the infinite to finite man a little more in detail. Since the dawn of philosophical thinking, man has been struggling to ascertain the ultimate essence of things, to learn something of the great reality which he felt lay behind the appearance of things. The endeavor to pierce the veil of phenomena or appearances and detect the noumenon, the thing itself as distinct from its manifestations, appearances or phenomena, has gone on from generation to generation. Theory after theory of the ultimate essence of things, the great first cause, absolute being, God, call the infinite power of the universe what you will, have been propounded, made followers, been discredited and become of mere historical interest. The most brilliant intellects the human race has brought forth have in the ages past devoted themselves to the fascinating study of ontology, the search after the nature of absolute being. The failure in this search of the most determined efforts of the giant minds of the past at last caused it to dawn on the philosophical intelligence that phenomena or the manifestations of the infinite power are the only legitimate objects of study of the human mind. The efforts of the metaphysician, in his search after the nature of absolute being, seem destined to be placed alongside the search of the alchemists after the secret of the transmutation of metals. We of the present day, while discarding the hopes of the metaphysician and the alchemist, inherit the great negative results of their labors. The tyro may smile at the indefatigable perseverance and the exhaustless enthusiasm of these searchers after the impossible, but had there been no alchemy there were now no chemistry, and the speculator on the ultimate essence of things in the past has made possible the philosophy of the present. The alchemist having made evident the impossibility of the transmutation of metals, the chemist now gives explanation of the fact; the ever varying and always contradictory results of the metaphysician having demonstrated the impossibility of defining the great first cause, the psychologist now gives the explanation and shows us why the very nature of our being renders it impossible to know anything whatsoever of the ultimate essence of things.

This explanation he for convenience has labeled the "relativity of knowledge." By this expression he intends to convey the idea that all we can know of things is the impressions they make upon ourselves. We really know nothing of even the simplest thing which presents itself to our notice, except the impressions it makes upon us. For example we say that the stone which lies at our feet is brown or gray, or yellow or green as the case may be, and yet this matter of color is the effect of the reflection from the stone upon the retina of the eye of certain rays of light which come not from the stone but from some luminous body. In the dark the stone has no color whatever. The old proverb that "all cats are black in the dark" formulates in popular language a scientific truth. The knowledge then of the color of the stone is merely an impression upon the mind. What real characteristic of the stone causes it to absorb certain of the rays of white light falling upon it and reflect others is unknown and probably ever will be. That the appearance of an object is merely an impression and is nothing more is proved by the work of skillful painters, who, with properly produced effects of light and shade, so simulate the impression produced upon the eye by the objects familiar to us that in many cases the illusion is perfect when viewed from the proper standpoint; sometimes only touch itself reveals the deception. The mirage is another familiar example of the lack of universality of the statement that "seeing is believing." The odors of bodies turn out upon investigation to be only the impression produced upon the olfactory nerves by particles of those bodies driven off by heat: when sufficient heat is lacking there is no odor. But coming to the most fundamental, and at the same time most certain means of knowledge—touch—we find that it furnishes once more only impressions. When we feel of an object presented to us, what we know is our own sensations only. The knowledge that the thing presented is hard or soft or round or square, upon investigation we find is merely the knowledge of the sensations conveyed through our nerves to the brain. The idea that the body is either heavy or light is the result of the sensation of muscular effort necessary to lift it. The characteristic of resistance, which is a necessary concomitant of all matter, is known to us only by the sensation produced within us by the muscular effort put forth by us to overcome it. That the body is in motion is again merely an impression, as is proved by the familiar experience of the impossibility of determining whether our own train or one in close proximity is slowly moving. Information regarding proximity or remoteness and of size are found to be due to multiplied impressions. When not assisted by means with which to gauge the distance, it is impossible for one to determine whether the object seen is a man further off or a boy near at hand. If on the other hand we know the distance is great we decide in favor of its being a man; if the contrary, the decision is in favor of its being a boy. When we feel of an object we declare it hot or cold, but the knowledge is only of sensations produced within ourselves, because as our own hand is warmer or cooler the object felt of seems cooler or warmer. The rug seems warm to the bare foot while the wood floor alongside seems cold, yet the temperature of both rug and floor may be the same. But every reader may multiply examples to show that all our knowledge of everything external to ourselves is relative to ourselves. That is to say, the only possible knowledge we can have of anything whatsoever is the impression which the thing produces upon us. We are conscious of something external to ourselves, and we are further conscious of the manner in which that something affects us. And this of necessity is all we can know, and it might be added all we need to know. The fact that if we had further senses we would be conscious of other activities in things about us; or the fact that things have myriads of possibilities of effects not appreciated by us; or that something which we know by one or a thousand effects may be producing a million which we cannot discern, is a matter of little consequence or even no consequence to us. Out of the infinity of possible activities or relationships of anything, the only ones which need give us any concern are those which relate to ourselves.

Since then all man's knowledge of things consists in a knowledge of their effects upon himself, since his knowledge of all things beyond himself must be expressed in terms of himself, he naturally and inevitably attributes to them somewhat of the characteristics of his own personality. In other words he *personifies* all things which come within the range

MYSTERY OF REVELATION 247

of his observation or thought. Uncultivated races or races in the early state of cultivation picture to themselves all things under the form of personality. Mountains, rivers, oceans, woods, trees, winds, weather, the heavenly bodies, the seasons and all things natural, material and immaterial, are known to them in terms of personality. This personification of the things of nature has been universal. Indeed, knowledge of them could be formulated only by resorting to personification. The immature intellect was conscious of ability to exert force to build up, to destroy, to remove, to be willing and unwilling to yield, to resist. These and similar notions, gathered from his own consciousness, became of necessity the only kind of terms in which he could represent anything to his consciousness.

Furthermore, the only way we may know anything is by noting its likeness or unlikeness to something else. We know a thing when we have observed it and compared it with the previously known, and classified it according to its likeness or unlikeness. We understand a new phenomenon when we have compared it with other phenomena, and on account of its likeness or unlikeness to other phenomena have classified it. The only way we may perceive any object is by noticing that it is different from other objects surrounding it. Our perception, for instance, of a tree depends upon our noting that it is unlike the meadow, the stream, the clouds and the other objects which occupy or have occupied the attention. This involves always comparison. But things in order to be compared must be reduced to common terms; there must be some common standard of comparison. Yards, rods, furlongs and miles can only be intelligently compared when all are reduced to the common terms of, say, feet, when the foot is used for the standard of comparison. Men and mountains do not permit of comparison ordinarily, but if measured by the common standard of greatness they admit of ready comparison. The mountain torrent and anger cannot ordinarily be compared together, but if destructiveness be used as the common measure they admit of relationship. Thus it has happened that the undeveloped man has been able to accumulate knowledge, by using as the common standard of comparison the only one within reach—his own personality. The works and operations of nature would have remained forever an unrelated jumble of observations had not man applied the magic wand of his own personality to bring order out of chaos, to turn perception into knowledge. The varying moods of the ocean, the wanderings of the river, the ever-changing weather, the murmuring streams, the harvest-producing earth, and the countless other manifestations of nature's forces, only became comprehensible when compared with man's own personality.

The means by which man built the foundations of knowledge are imbedded in his language. Peasant and philosopher still say *it* rains, *it* snows, *it* will be fair or foul. The highly cultivated designer, the master builder, and the meanest ignoramus in the watching crowd, would all alike state, when the great ship remained upon the stays in spite of every effort to launch her into the water, that she *refused* to move, that she *resisted* all their efforts. Whence results the expression of chemical *affinity* except from the personification of the chemical elements? How can any professor bring home to the minds of his class the one distinguishing characteristic of nitrogen more speedily and effectually than by saying it is an unsociable element? We speak of the smiling fields and gloomy forests, the angry waves, the sullen roar of the surf, the pitiless sea, and in numberless other forms of speech tacitly admit the ineradicable and necessary habit of personification of nature's works and forces. As the immature races, so also the immature individuals build up their knowledge by the ever-ready and only available instrument, personification. Every one recalls the manner in which young children inject their own personalities into inanimate things. The door which pinches the finger or the chair against which the head has been bumped are wicked and blameworthy. Many a weeping child has been stilled by a whipping administered to some offending door or chair. The dogs and the cats are at first not strongly differentiated, either from the toys on the one side or human beings on the other, by the child. The qualities of all things external are so closely identified with the personal medium through which knowledge of them is obtained, that only countless succeeding impressions show the faultiness of the earlier impressions. As comparisons succeed each other in infinite number and variety, the external world is more and more differentiated from the personality of the observer. Whether in the case of the race or the individual, as the observations multiply a process of de-personification goes on. As knowledge increases and as relationships multiply, and as the relationships between exter-

MYSTERY OF REVELATION 251

nal things are observed, the mind becomes equipped with standards of comparison less and less imbued with the personality of the observer. The mature and cultivated man of to-day no longer needs to regard the winds, rivers, seas and woods as persons endowed with human personalities. He has largely de-personified them.

But even the highest developed intellect still needs to resort to tacit, if not avowed personification if he would effectively bring home to his intelligence composite feelings and thoughts. The sailor personifies his ship and in speaking of it uses the pronoun of the feminine gender. To the stranger the vessel may be represented to the mind by the pronoun *it*, but to the master whom she has carried safely through many a storm, and to whose will she has responded as a thing alive, to whom she stands for pride and duty, and who loves her in very deed, the word *it* applied to his ship would seem as inappropriate as if applied to his wife. The clustering ideas and feelings absolutely require personification for their adequate representation to his mind. The square miles of territory, the woods, rivers and lakes, the cities and towns of a nation may be represented to the mind of the observer without resort to personification; but when the idea of the nation which calls forth sentiments of love and patriotism is to be presented to the mind, we must needs again resort to personification. The patriot regards his country as a person who observes, praises, blames, honors, condemns, suffers and rejoices; and he is compelled so to do by the constitution of his being.

The lower man's intelligence the more he likens external things to sides of his own personality. When he does not move when influenced so to do, he refuses to move or is unwilling to move, and therefore the inanimate object which under pressure does not move he can best understand as refusing or being unwilling to move. He has a clear conception of the state of affairs by likening the immovable thing to his knowledge of himself under similar circumstances. Even the most educated man has a more vivid impression of the violence of the waves when he puts the color of his own personality into the picture and thinks of them as angry. The sea which in spite of all endeavor engulfs the ship is better represented to poet and peasant when it is conceived of as a creature, pitiless, remorseless, insatiable, although these are strictly personal attributes. What is needed by the mind is the exact representation of the reality, and this representation, contradictory as it may seem, is often to be obtained only by resort to ideality. So we find that personification is not only the first instrument used in the gathering of knowledge, but it is to the end an essential instrument.

If it be objected that personification is a source of error, it may be replied that instrumentalities are good when they answer the purpose for which they are designed; knowledge is accurate when it suffices for the proper guidance of the one possessing it. The railway guide-map is accurate if it shows the termini and the general course of the road represented, although it may not be correct in a single detail as compared with the engineering map used in operating the road. The railroad time-table map is meant to convey certain information to the traveling public, for this purpose it is accurate, correct and true. The carpenter's rule can be said to be correct and true though not a single division upon it corresponds with the standards, if it suffices for building purposes. And so a statement of fact or a theory may be both true and false according as viewed from one standpoint or another. Truth of statement does not always consist in exact correspondence with fact. Indeed, a most adroit lie may be in exact accordance with fact. A man who is asked if he was at the corner of A and X streets at six o'clock on a certain day may reply "No" if he were a yard away at six o'clock or was passing the corner a second before or after, and yet for the purposes of the inquiry not be stating the truth. On the contrary, for the purposes of the inquiry the true answer would be "Yes," although not in correspondence with the exact facts of the case. Truth of impression and truth of statement do not always correspond. For the purposes of daily life it is true to say that the sun set at such a time, although astronomically considered the statement is absolutely untrue. Every school text-book is full of misstatements concerning the exact truth, measured by scientific rules of exactness, yet true knowledge is conveyed by them. Every lecturer on science to popular audiences continually finds himself under the necessity of sacrificing scientific exactness to popular comprehension. All that can be required is that his statements shall be in the line of complete truth. Man must learn the truth by degrees; the partial statements made to the beginner must be abandoned by the scholar, not that they are untrue but because they are incomplete. Incompleteness becomes untruth only when out of harmony with its surroundings. It is not improper to acquiesce in a personification of the impersonal while this leads to the comprehension of the natural things, although of course the teacher is aware of its falsity in fact. As man gains knowledge of nature so he gains knowledge of God —not all at once, but by steps: the knowledge in the beginning is as incomplete as his intellectual capacity is limited. Accuracy of comprehension and not exactness of detail is what should be looked for, and upon investigation what is found.

Let us now examine the anthropomorphological character of Christianity in connection with the principle of relativity of knowledge and man's necessary habit of personification. Our knowledge of God must be like our knowledge of all else, relative merely; that is, we can know absolutely nothing of the nature of God except as transmitted through and modified by the medium of our own personality. But we certainly can have knowledge of God just as we have knowledge of the forces of nature, by knowing his manifestations. If we cannot know the real nature of God, neither can we know the real nature of the physical universe; if we can only know the phenomena of nature, we certainly may know the phenomena or manifestations which God makes to man. If it be of no practical consequence that we cannot arrive at any knowledge whatever of the ultimate essence of things physical, it is of no more consequence that we are barred from knowing the real nature of God's being. If it suffices us to know phenomena, and know nothing of the great reality behind the phenomena, except that it exists and manifests itself by the phenomena, it should suffice us to know God as he has manifested himself to us, albeit he be, as he himself has declared, past finding out. All that we need know concerning God is his relationship to us, that is to say, the manner in which he manifests himself to us. If we cannot conceive of God as an absolute being what matters it? Neither can we conceive of the absolute power behind phenomena. If it be philosophical and sensible to give over the attempt to discover the reality behind phenomena, and concern ourselves only with the phenomena themselves, so it is philosophical, sensible, and also scriptural, to leave the absolute nature of God where he has left it, in impenetrable and unfathomable mystery, and concern ourselves only with the phenomena, appearances or revelations of God.

MYSTERY OF REVELATION 257

While noting that knowledge is limited to phenomena, we note also that it is a growth. It is always continuous. What we learn to-day must of necessity be built upon the experiences of yesterday and the days before. Experiences may only be understood or comprehended by us when we are able to compare and classify them with previous experiences. This comparison involves measurable likeness or similarity; therefore it is that we must always begin with the rudiments of any branch of knowledge or science, because the rudiments or roots of all kinds of knowledge are similar. We can always grasp or comprehend the rudiments of a new department of knowledge because these rudiments are so like our previous knowledge as to admit of comparison. The rudiments of the new knowledge having been added to our experience, facts and principles, similar to but differing from those preceding them in our experience, are continuously added, until at length we grasp and make our own, by means of this continuous line of comparison and classification, things so different from our original experience that they would originally have been impossible of comparison and therefore of comprehension.

So must knowledge of God, though it be

gained by a revelation, be a growth; and in the beginning it must be of a nature admitting of comparison with the existing knowledge or experience of the individual to whom it is made. But because it is incomplete it need never be untrue. The conception of God, by the ripest theological scholar, is not, upon introspection, found by him to antagonize or be inconsistent with the ideas of the time when first he learned the simple "Now I lay me down to sleep" of the child's prayer. Of course his conceptions are vastly extended, but without the rudimentary knowledge fitted to the experience of his childish years his present theological conceptions would be an impossibility. The rudiments, whether they be of geology or theology, must ever precede "advanced ideas." In every case the knowledge of God must be adjusted to the experience, the knowledge of the individual possessing it. The personification of God is on this account an inherent necessity of revelation; and furthermore, the personification must be the more approximated to the human personality, the younger and more inexperienced the individual or the race to whom it is to be made. As man could in the beginning only obtain knowledge of nature by endowing its works and forces with almost perfect human personality, so has human nature required a similar personification of God. Starting with what to riper experience seems a gross personification, man as a race and as an individual comes to differentiate nature more and more from himself. The personal element grows less and less as experience is added unto experience. As the revelation of nature to man has developed, so has the revelation of God. In the beginning the knowledge of God must be very near akin to man's own personality; as experience increases, as the horizon expands, as the grasp of the things of the universe becomes stronger, as the relationship in his environment becomes more clearly comprehended, man differentiates God more and more from man. But these later, and as they seem to us more complete ideas of God, can only come to each individual and to each race through the same process of personification; the rudimentary knowledge must ever be the same.

Nor must we fail to note that both the revelation of nature and the revelation of God to man have always been sufficient to enable him to properly adjust himself to his environment; have always been graduated so as to harmonize with the various stages of his general development, have always accorded with the capacities of its recipient. The revelation has thus been, in a way, always complete; and the impression produced has, in its broad outlines, been ever the same. The possession of five hundred dollars or five million dollars are in themselves exceedingly different, yet the impression of wealth produced by this possession may be in different persons exactly the same, and if the object of the bestowal of money be to produce a conception of wealth, the one sum may be as adequate as the other under the varying conditions of destitution and opulence; so the object of revelation being a knowledge of the relationship of God to man, the revelation to Abraham may have been as efficacious as the revelation to Peter, yet the revelation in the one case must have been very different from that in the other. But that which produced such vivid and effectual impressions upon the minds of the apostles would have been incomprehensible, doubtless, to the more limited experience of Abraham, Isaac and Jacob. The knowledge of God communicated to the race by Christ could not, upon the principles previously noted, have been comprehended in advance of the rudiments previously communicated to the race. The Sermon on the Mount and the theological ideas of John and Paul could no more have been grasped by the race in advance of the experiences of the Jewish people, than the evolutionary philosophy of the present day could have been understood by Newton or Bacon in advance of the chemical, physical and biological experience of later years. But, as it may well be doubted whether the glory and power of nature affect the mind of the latter-day philosopher any more profoundly than they impressed the minds of Newton, Herschel or Young; or, comparatively speaking, it may be doubtful whether the fuller revelation to the apostles revealed any more fully the power and glory of God to them than they were revealed to Moses and David. But the impressions produced upon the philosopher of the eighteenth century cannot be produced upon the philosopher of the nineteenth century by means of the same knowledge, because the proportions are destroyed by the vast advancement in learning in these latter days. The sensations produced upon the childish mind by the donation of a penny can only be produced later on by the donation of a pound, and later on by perhaps a thousand of them. So the appreciation of God's relationship to man could only be brought home to the human race in the Christian era by a revelation adjusted to the advancement of the race.

Since in all cases, then, the object of revelation is to reveal, and the revealing must always of necessity be adjusted to the individual to whom the revelation is to be made, it must be to the undeveloped and the immature intensely anthropomorphological. It must be formulated in terms admitting of comparison with the then accumulated experiences of the individual or the race. If in the days of the Israelites God "came down," "visited," "determined," "repented," was "angry" and "pleased"; if he "dwelt among them" and "departed from them," and in general manifested himself to them as possessed of intensely human characteristics, what of it? This is just what in the nature of things we should expect; in no other terms could God have manifested his relationship to them; in such terms of humanity alone could he reveal himself. We, with advancing experience, have indeed outgrown some of these ultra-anthropomorphological conceptions, but after all we are still dependent upon anthropomorphological methods of thought. Although the Christian conception of God's relationship is immeasurably less humanized than that of the Israelites of old, still we shall doubtless never outgrow our dependence upon the idea of fatherhood and brotherhood, in conceiving of

MYSTERY OF REVELATION 263

the relationship of God and Christ towards man. We have spiritualized to an almost inconceivable degree our ideas of God, but as long as we remain human we must ever formulate our ideas of God as of all things else, in terms of humanity; and this must be so even though in larger measure, we being spirits, spiritually discern God, the Father of our spirits. Even though spiritual faculties discern spiritual qualities, nevertheless in the expression of spiritual knowledge even to ourselves we must depend upon human means, just as the mind, whose existence of a surety cannot be denied, is forced to depend for expression upon physiological means. What mind is, is as inscrutable a mystery as the Great Unknown behind the phenomena of nature; but for conception and expression it is confined to the instrumentality of physiological combinations. It is therefore entirely in accordance with our experience if the spirit be under the necessity of reliance upon things human to conceive of and express things spiritual.

The mystery of religion, like the mystery of nature, is so profound, so impossible of comprehension, that Christ used no mere figure of speech when he said, " Whosoever shall not receive the kingdom of God as a little child, he shall in nowise enter therein." Those who will not approach the mystery of nature and the mystery of godliness in the spirit of children will never enter. They may gain certain distorted visions of these kingdoms, but, lacking genuine humility, they are without the key which opens the gate. The characteristics which must belong to the searcher after truth, be it natural or religious, are beautifully set forth by that prince of natural philosophers, Michael Faraday. He says: "The philosopher should be a man willing to listen to every suggestion, but determined to judge for himself. He should not be biased by appearances, have no favorite hypothesis, be of no school, and in doctrine have no master. He should not be a respecter of persons, but of things. Truth should be his primary object. If to these qualities be added industry, he may indeed hope to walk within the veil of the temple of nature. We may be sure of facts, but our interpretation of facts we should doubt. He is the wisest philosopher who holds his theory with some doubt. Nothing is more difficult and requires more care than philosophical deduction, nor is there anything more adverse to its accuracy than fixity of opinion. The man who is certain he is right is almost sure to be wrong, and he has the additional misfortune of inevitably remaining so." It was the opinion of Faraday that man must enter the kingdom of nature even as he must enter the kingdom of heaven—as a child. The child adds to his knowledge day by day, undeterred, undismayed by the infinite unknowable. He is uninfluenced by, nay almost regardless of what lies beyond the range of his experience. The value of his finite knowledge is not diminished by the infinity of his ignorance. But if the unknown dampens not the ardor of his search after new knowledge, neither in him does knowledge become a preventive of further knowledge; neither his ignorance nor his knowledge checks his restless inquiry into the nature of things; to him nothing is strange and to him all things are wonderful. Unconsciously the child never pits his limited experience against the infinite possibilities of things; to him, whatever is can be. In maturer years the temptation is almost irresistible to reverse this; so that he comes to act upon the principle that only what in the light of his experience can be, is. According to Faraday, this last condition of mind is fatal to advance in the acquisition of scientific knowledge; the Scriptures tell us it is equally fatal to the acquisition of religious truth. Only those who grasp the principle involved in the saying, "With man it is impossible, but not with God: for all things are possible with God," can hope to walk within the veil of the temple of nature, or to enter the kingdom of God. One who approaches any avenue of knowledge with preconceived ideas of possibility and impossibility, founded upon that philosophical deduction declared to be difficult by such a past master in the art as Faraday, carries with him an effectual bar to even entering therein.

CHAPTER XIV

THE REASONABLENESS OF THE REVELATION OF LIFE

What God might have done it is impossible to say, but what God has done is to establish man's reason as the Court of Appeals in all matters pertaining to man. Among these matters pertaining to man, certainly the most important are things religious—the relationship of God to man.

It is contended by many good and wise men, that since the nature of God is beyond man's comprehension, since God is infinite and man finite, religion cannot be left to the acceptance or rejection of man's reason. While admitting the jurisdiction of the court of reason in all else, they deny its jurisdiction in all such matters as the revelation of the Scriptures and of so-called religious doctrines. But as we have seen, the argument of such is just as applicable to the things of nature as the things of religion. The physical universe and the forces controlling it are infinite, and utterly beyond comprehension by the mind of man. If the things of religion are not to be submitted to man's reason because of the infinity of the God of religion, then neither can the things of nature be submitted to man's reason because of the infinity of the powers of nature.

Without wandering into the realms of abstract philosophy, we may find, in the region of practical experience, the refutation of the idea that man's reason is not a court of general jurisdiction over things religious as well as things natural. When the missionary goes to the peoples who know not the God of Abraham, Isaac and Jacob, and who have no knowledge of Christ or his apostles, to what does he appeal? To the ordinary reasoning powers of his hearers. This appeal must of necessity be his very first step. Does he ground his teaching upon the Scriptures, he must needs then first give some account of their production and transmission. Does he rely upon the mere propounding of the truth itself, and rely upon its acceptance because it is true, without regard to the authority of its original promulgation, then he must show how it harmonizes with other knowledge of truth already possessed, how it satisfies natural longings, how it is adjusted to the constitution of human nature. In every case he must follow the example set by God himself, through his prophet Isaiah, when he said, "Come let us reason together." In every case he must teach and preach, persuade and convince; and all these things of necessity involve argument, reasoning on the part of the one propounding the truth, and involve the exercise of the faculty of reason by the one accepting or mayhap rejecting the truth propounded. The same appeal to reason must be made in the inculcation of religious truth in children. Until the child has arrived at such a stage of experience as to admit of reasoning, the presentation of religious ideas is not possible. It receives knowledge of God as it receives knowledge of nature, by the process of comparison and classification. Knowledge of God can no more be acquired without the aid of these processes than the knowledge of natural phenomena. The thousand and one inquiries propounded by the child relative to the nature of God and his dealings with man, show conclusively the train of reasoning concerning these things carried on by it.

The process employed in teaching and learning religious things is indistinguishable from the process employed in learning natural things. The sole method of separating truth from error is by the process of reasoning. The acceptance or rejection of anything as true or false depends upon the exercise of judgment, which is the result or final state of a process of reasoning. The whole Bible from Genesis to Revelation is but one grand appeal to man's judgment or reason, and it is hard to imagine whence the modern heresy that God ordinarily appeals to man otherwise than through his reasoning powers has arisen.

That spiritual man, having been born again into a new kingdom, and having thus become endowed with ultra-human faculties, is enabled to know something of God, unattainable by unassisted reason, is not disputed but affirmed. But the necessary preparation for the new birth depends, as has been seen, upon man. The influences within and without, which effect this preparation can only be brought to bear by constant appeals to the reasoning faculties of man. But not even after the birth of the new creature can this new creature become independent of the human faculty of reason, any more than the intangible mind can become independent of physiological unit and chemical combinations. The human is as intimately identified with the spiritual, and as necessary for the exercise of its functions, as the material is intimately connected with and necessary for the exercise of the functions of the mental. In a word, it is impossible to conceive how religious truth can be brought home to the human being except through the exercise of reason. The truth is never dangerous except to those who oppose it; and it will be found that no damage accrues to religion in meeting its critics on their own ground and admitting the fact that it must plead in the court of reason and submit to its judgment.

Is, then, Christianity with its revelation of the new spirit life reasonable or unreasonable? Upon analysis it is found that, both in the language of science and the language of everyday life, that is reasonable which accords with experience. As we have seen, the acquisition of knowledge is a growth; therefore each additional element is intimately associated with what has immediately preceded it. Each new element of knowledge will be different from, but must be also very similar to, some element before acquired; it must be sufficiently harmonious with something that has preceded it in experience to render it capable of being joined to it: in other words, it must harmonize with experience. If new material for the increase of knowledge be presented to the mind which is very dissimilar to knowledge already acquired, it cannot be assimilated and does not become understood or known. When some principle of trigonometry or calculus is presented to the mind ignorant of the elements of mathematics, the principle is incapable of assimilation; it is too dissimilar to the elements of knowledge already acquired to admit of comparison and classification and being joined to the body of knowledge. This of course follows from the fact that knowledge only grows by a classification of the likenesses or unlikenesses of the new to the old—in other words, by reasoning. Hence when the newly presented matter is so dissimilar to previous experience as to be incapable of comparison with it, it is said to be unreasonable, that is to say it is incapable of being joined to the existing fabric of knowledge by the necessary process of reasoning.

Having thus noted that those things are reasonable which correspond with experience, and that the unreasonable is that which is contrary to experience, let us inquire into the nature of the experience required as a standard. The experience frequently and erroneously relied upon as a test of reasonableness is one's own individual experience, yet the constant teaching of personal experience is its unreliability as a sole test for what is reasonable or unreasonable. The admonitions of older people relative to the dangers of unripe fruit do not at first seem reasonable to the infant. It is not in accordance with the experience of infancy that harm can follow the eating of anything that is pleasant to the taste; only after sad experiences of suffering does the connection between colic and unripe fruit accord with personal experience and seem reasonable. The warnings of Washington to General Braddock and his officers were to them unreasonable in the highest degree. These men had plenty of experience in war, and the statements of the young colonist were rejected because they did not accord with this experience, and were thus seemingly unreasonable. To the survivors of the ill-fated expedition, the statements of Washington relative to Indian warfare accorded with their experience and were reasonable to a degree. Only after many bitter lessons does the ordinary mortal learn that although that which is reasonable must accord with experience, he must look beyond himself for the experience with which the accord is necessary. The reasonable man, that is to say the man who acts in accordance with experience, depends in the ordinary affairs of life far more upon the recognized experience of others than upon his own. In the preparation of his food, in the manufacture of his clothing, in the conduct of his business, in his recourse to physician and lawyer, he finds many unreasonable things, if judged only by his personal experience. Therefore the conception of the reasonable as that which conforms to experience must be broadened so as to include what we believe to be the experience of others as well as ourselves. But even this broadening of the range of experience will not suffice; we act upon many an occasion in a manner which the results justify without the assistance of any known experience of ourselves or others. Powerful instincts often safely guide us into conformity with novel surroundings; we call this instinctive action reasonable because we "feel" it so. But in these cases we are served by the inherited experience of countless ancestors. Many actions which would be unreasonable if they needed to be justified by known experience, are reasonable when judged by the standard of the experience of the race. Thus the very highest overshadowing teaching of experience is the unreasonableness of finally rejecting any matter brought before us as unreasonable because it is beyond our present personal experience. The very doctrine that the reasonable is that which is in harmony with experience demands that we must often accept as reasonable that which is beyond our own personal experience.

When about to advance into the regions of the unknown for the acquisition of new knowledge, the investigator usually has recourse to analogy to determine the direction in which he should proceed. This is simply a determining what would be reasonable if discovered; that is to say, a determination, upon the inspection of previous experience, of what would harmonize with it. It is a well-known maxim that no analogy goes on all fours. This briefly puts the principle heretofore dwelt upon, that in the reasonable we do not look for unison, but harmony. We look for that which may be fitted into our experience on one or more sides, always leaving one or more sides differing entirely from anything heretofore built into the fabric of knowledge. Every investigator is aware of the fact that many of the best additions to knowledge have come from pursuing faint analogies. That is to say, the new element has gone almost to the verge of contradiction of previous experience. As we have seen, some similarity, however slight, must invariably exist between the new and the old; but, like the grain of mustard seed in the parable, it need be but very small. We have learned by experience that among the possibilities of the unknown that is the more likely to be true which fits our experience on most sides, and we call such a thing probable; but it not infrequently happens that the improbable, the things which touch and fit experience at few points are true. Widening experience, however, shows that the improbable which turned out to be true fits accurately newly added elements of knowledge, whereas that which before seemed probable would have been incapable of adjustment to new elements as the building of knowledge went on. Thus even apparent failures of experience as the test of the reasonable and the true, in the end established but the more strongly its sole availability. The failures always arise, not from defect in the standard, but in our present lack of knowledge of it. Limited experience is the necessary and sufficient guide to further experience; and as experience is added to experience and knowledge expands we find order evolving out of chaos, certainty emerging from doubt, and the truth standing out at last clear and distinct.

The stones of the edifice of truth are ready

cut to our hand, but all unmarked; what has been done in the past is the only guide to the work of the future, and the building is therefore slow. Many a stone is used in the wrong place because of seeming fitness, only afterwards to be extricated from its place at the expense of tearing down much that is associated with it. The proper stone in the proper place will fit or harmonize not only with those before built into the walls, but with all those which must thereafter be built about it. The reasonable must not only fit experience past but experience future. The truth will not only harmonize with what has been but what shall be. But as the building of knowledge progresses, the only possible method of procedure is to daily add the things which may be true in the light of past experience, trusting that the future will decide that the builder has not determined amiss. What is reasonable, what is probable, is man's only guide to truth, whether it be in choosing a road, erecting a building, constructing a science, or seeking the kingdom of heaven.

Bearing in mind then that those things are reasonable which harmonize with experience, and that those things only are unreasonable which are incapable of being fitted to experience, and that the law of growth shows that a new element of knowledge need only accord with previous knowledge or experience on one side, let us test the revelations of the Scriptures by this standard of the reasonable. It will be found in all cases that the teachings proceeding from the Creator are not out of harmony with the receptive faculties of the creature—that they are addressed to his reason.

The comparison, here, of scriptural teachings with the fruits of experience must of necessity be limited to a few points. One of the most striking inferences from human experience is the vastness of the change which must of necessity take place in the environment of the human being at death. Indeed, so incalculably great is this change supposed to be that very many cannot conceive how individuality can survive it. But if the survival be possible, our experience teaches that the being surviving must be capable of adjusting itself to the changes of the environment, and that the capacity for adjustment must be great in proportion to the greatness of the change.

Given the environment, the naturalist has little difficulty in deciding upon the general characteristics of the creature capable of life within it. This follows from the principle that life is the correspondence of an organism with its environment; and this correspondence involves perceptions, powers and instrumentalities in the organism rendering it possible. The creature furnished with gills but without lungs could not correspond with the environment of the atmosphere. Neither could the animal with lungs and no gills or equivalent organs live in the water; taken from the air and immersed in the water, the change in its environment would be such as to destroy life because of inability to adjust itself to its new surroundings. Changes like these are so great that they demand a greater capacity for adjustment than the organism possesses, correspondence ceases, and death results. Smaller changes in the environment involve less capacity to change in the organism living in it. But in all cases a change in the environment involves an equivalent change in the organism if life is to continue. Therefore the naturalist deduces the general rule that every organism must be furnished with organs and be capable of performing functions to correspond with its environment; that changed environment demands different organs or the exercise of different functions; and that the greater the difference in the environment the greater the difference in the characteristics of the living beings within it.

If the characteristics of the environment be unknown, the characteristics of the living being inhabiting it cannot be inferred; but if it be known that a certain environment is very different from other known environments, it may be predicted with certainty that the beings living in that environment must have characteristics widely different from those living in the known environments. If it be granted, then, that the environment after death is fundamentally different from anything with which we are acquainted, it must likewise be admitted that the beings capable of life in that environment must be essentially different from the ordinary beings of the human race. This is the teaching of science or experience, and this is the exact and literal teaching of the New Testament Scriptures, which set forth the absolute necessity of a new creature to make possible the inheritance or obtaining of eternal life. According to our experience, new creatures must be *born*, and again this is the exact declaration of the Scriptures. The new creature, as we have seen, should be essentially and fundamentally different from the human being of the present environment, and this again the Scriptures declare to be the true doctrine. Therefore the scriptural teaching that the human being

THE REVELATION OF LIFE 281

is destined to death, that the only possibility of the survival of the individual is the development within him of a new creature, by a new birth, possessed of new faculties, new powers, new perceptions, is harmonious with experience—is reasonable.

As to the existence of a new environment differing from all present known environments, this is reasonable, because we know from experience that the known is infinitesimally small, and that in the unknown there are infinite possibilities, so that the fact of the existence of a condition of things differing from that with which we are acquainted is reasonable, is probable. As regards the existence of living beings in this unknown universe, beyond our range of ordinary perception, all that is required to make it reasonable is that it shall not be negatived by experience. Observing the different orders of things in the visible universe and noting that they ascend from mineral to plant, from plant to animal, from animal to man; and observing that the existence of each higher order depends in nowise on the perception of that order by those below it, or upon the lower order possessing the faculties necessary for this perception, it may be asserted without fear of contradiction that the existence of an order superior to man is in entire harmony with experience as far as it has extended. The positive declaration of the Scriptures as to the existence of a kingdom of heaven, higher than any of the kingdoms of earth, where a new condition of things prevails, and where new and, to human beings, unknown forces hold sway, is not incapable of being fitted to our present knowledge. It is in line with the trend of present experience; and the further declaration that the members of this kingdom are living beings endowed with personality and individuality is harmonious with the teachings of science, with formulated experience, with reason.

The study of the different kingdoms reveals a connection between the lower and the higher. Each higher order is dependent for its existence upon the lower. The members of each higher kingdom are dependent for their organs and for the exercise of their functions upon the materials furnished by the lower. The plant life cannot exist separate and apart from its mineral associate elements; the germ of life contained in the seed exists only by virtue of the mineral elements so mysteriously associated with it. When it germinates into a plant, the plant grows only by appropriating to itself the mineral elements

THE REVELATION OF LIFE 283

of air and soil surrounding it. It is impossible to separate the plant life from the silica and potash, the nitrogen and the carbon which make it possible. Ascending the scale, we find animal life appropriating to itself the prepared elements of vegetable life, either directly from the plant kingdom or indirectly through some other animal which has before secured them from that kingdom. As it is ordinarily expressed, the plants live upon the minerals, and the animals live upon the plants. The animal is thus doubly indebted to both the mineral and the plant kingdom for its existence; it cannot do without the elements furnished by the mineral kingdom, nor yet can it obtain these necessary elements directly from that kingdom. Regarding man as belonging to a yet higher kingdom than the animal, we find still the same law holding good. Those faculties possessed by man and those functions performed by him which distinguish him from the animal are only possible through the animal elements of his composite being. He can only reason by virtue of the physiological part of him. That mind is a thing apart from the anatomical organs and physiological functions through and by means of which it manifests itself and exercises power, is the opinion of the ripest psychological scholarship of to-day. But no psychologist or theologian would think for one moment of denying the impossibility of the development, growth and exercise of mental powers apart from the physiological cell or the organic proteids. The member of the human kingdom therefore is triply indebted to the kingdoms below; he is dependent upon the mineral elements and upon the plant and the animal. Nor can the intellect which distinguishes him be produced or exercise itself without the joint agency of mineral, plant and animal. If then depending upon known experience we should inquire concerning the probable nature of a being of a higher order than man, we should expect to find that being dependent upon and intimately connected with the kingdoms below; we should expect to find a being dependent for original creation, for growth and for the exercise of its powers upon man, the next lower order of creature, and through man upon the kingdoms below him; we should expect to find a being having an element within him existing as a thing distinct from and yet dependent upon the human element; and we should further expect to find that this new separate and distinct entity, this new thing apart, influenced, nay sometimes controlled by the

THE REVELATION OF LIFE

lower elements with which it is indissolubly united. As the mind not only cannot exist separated from its material associates, but is under the dominion to a large degree of heat and cold, and food and drink, things of the mineral and plant kingdoms, and digestion, and waste and decay, affecting the animal frame; so we should expect the spiritual creature to be not only dependent upon, but largely controlled by the human body and mind. All these distinguishing characteristics foreshadowed by our experience are found set forth in stated terms in the Scriptures. What our experience indicates the spiritual being should be the Scriptures declare that he is; and therefore the description of the nature of the new creature of the Scriptures is reasonable—it is in harmony with our experience.

Biology teaches not only that life proceeds always from life, that the dead never brings forth the living, but it also teaches that the new life is like that whence it proceeds. From human beings therefore we should obtain only human beings; human life can propagate only its own, varying, to be sure, but always human. We are, moreover, taught that the living organism generated must be brought into existence with faculties enabling it to correspond with its environment, otherwise life becomes impossible. Eggs hatched under water would not grow into birds; fish spawn without water would not develop into swimming fish. The organism must be born with a nature fitted to its prospective surroundings. Only the living creatures from the given environment can generate the organisms which will develop the characteristics necessary for correspondence with that environment. A creature to live under water must be given its life by fish; the creature to fly through the air must owe its being to the bird. Therefore experience would indicate that a creature capable of corresponding with the environment beyond the earthly kingdoms, beyond the physical and within the spiritual, must receive its life from the spiritual, from beyond man and his limited environment. This teaching of experience is the teaching of the Scriptures, for it is written that unless a man be born from above, born of the spirit, he cannot enter the kingdom of heaven.

All higher forms of life, as science declares, result from the union of two life-currents. The new creature of the new kingdom should therefore result from union of two life principles. But though different they should not, according to physiological principles, be too different, and therefore the two kinds of life must be brought into some degree of similarity, and these teachings of science are found to be the doctrine of the Scriptures. The life of man and the life of the spirit flow together in the production of the new spiritual creature, but the human life must be elevated to the point of possible union of the two.

So it seems beyond dispute that the existence of the spiritual kingdom, its great difference from the lower kingdoms, the necessity of the birth of a new creature capable of a new life within it, the new creature's dependence upon and intimate union with the human being, that the life of this new creature should come from beyond the human kingdom, that this new creature should result from the union of two kinds of life and should unite the characteristics of both, all of which are the teachings of the Scriptures, are in harmony with the experience of the human race and therefore reasonable.

These teachings likewise find support from the law of continuity. A fundamental teaching of science is that nature never leaps. Her progress is marked by a line without a break; all things graduate the one into the other; all things are continuous. Man for the sake of the acquisition of knowledge establishes divisions, but they exist only in the imagination. We have chemistry, geology, astronomy, mathematics, physics and metaphysics, science and art, theory and practice, matter and force, motion and rest, daylight and darkness, but no man can mark out the boundaries between them. This great law of continuity, one of the ripe fruits of experience, would demand that there should be no break between the human and the spiritual, but that the one should be continuous with the other; and this reasonable condition we find satisfied to the fullest extent by the scriptural teachings. Not only is entrance into the heavenly kingdom found through the human kingdom, but the powers of God manifested in the signs, works and wonders of the Scriptures, when found superior to, are intimately connected and associated with the ordinary powers of nature as we know them. Christ came not to destroy, but to fulfill, to go beyond the known indeed, but still in harmony with it.

The Scriptures teach also that which we have noted to be in accord with the highest experience, viz., the necessity of depending upon the experience, the testimony of others, as well as ourselves. What progress would science ever have made had no one ever been willing to depend upon the statements of others' experiences, or rely upon the results worked out by another mind. Planets, stars, comets, nebulae, upon which have depended great results, have been taken upon the faith of a very few astronomical observers; chemical analysis depends upon a sensitiveness of sight and smell possessed only by trained observers, yet their statements are accepted even to the point of life and death; the strange tales of travelers are proverbial, yet they have been none the less true; musical harmonies and discords are none the less real because not discoverable by all people, but the statements of those discerning them are not disbelieved, even by those who have never been able to hear them. How unreasonable, how contrary to and out of harmony with universal experience is it, therefore, for one to deny the reality of knowledge and experience, asserted to have been possessed by an innumerable host of most competent and truthful witnesses, because these experiences are not within the knowledge of all. It were the part of reason and of wisdom not to deny the reality of so-called Christian experience simply because it is not yet a matter of personal experience with all men.

But after all the keystone of the arch of human experience, the one great unvarying reliance in all human conduct, is the uniformity of the laws of nature. Consciously or unconsciously, every act and thought in the lives of men, be they peasants or princes, ignorant or learned, savage or civilized, is governed by reliance upon uniformity of law. So firmly has this reliance upon the uniformity of the laws of nature been fixed in our natures, by the cumulative experience of hundreds of generations of men, that anything contrary to it, or seemingly so, has the highest possible warrant of unreasonableness which can be furnished to our minds. The unprejudiced examiner will therefore apply this test of the reasonable to the teachings of the Scriptures with no little anxiety, and will arise from the consideration of it with a light heart when he discovers that only the misinterpretations of unwise friends and vicious foes have found anything contrary to this great principle of the uniformity of law in the Scriptures.

A volume would need to be written to show the fallacy of every one of these misinterpretations, but the general principle that God governs by fixed laws and not by caprice is so plainly set forth in the Scriptures that even he who runs may read, if he be only content to read the book as a whole and not pin his

THE REVELATION OF LIFE 291

opinion to isolated texts. For the purposes of the present argument it is only intended to refer to that one great doctrine which runs through the whole Bible, but is particularly enforced by Christ and his apostles, viz., that there is only one narrow unvarying way of life, and that failure to follow it, whatever be the excuses, means death. This doctrine of the Scriptures is in exact conformity with the trust in the uniformity of law grounded in experience. That which makes man's ordinary life possible, obedience to law, is found to be the principle involved in the teaching of Christ concerning the new life. In things natural man does not think it reasonable to disobey the self-announced laws of the universe because he cannot comprehend them. It is deemed in the highest degree reasonable for one to address himself diligently to the discovery of the laws of the infinitely great and varied forces in activity about him, and then with care to adjust his conduct in conformity with them. Therefore does it become man as a reasonable creature to give diligence to the search after the truth concerning the laws of human death and spiritual life, and then above all things else to give heed that he obeys them. If it be claimed by responsible witnesses that there is evidence of the life eternal, and that the law regarding it is capable of ascertainment, the gravity of the issue should allow none but a fool to refrain from an examination of the matter. And one should be vastly encouraged in the examination by finding that eternal life is not the result of caprice, is not a matter of sentiment, but depends upon inexorable, unvarying laws.

Christ came into the world not to judge, not to distribute rewards and punishments, as these are ordinarily understood, but to reveal the law of life. Those who, believing in him, follow his revelation and do his will, shall find themselves in the way of eternal life and receive it. Those who believe him not, and therefore heed him not, will know neither of the life nor the way to it. These will need no special judgment; the infinite, inscrutable, inexorable laws of the universe, both the seen and the unseen, will work out their swift and sure destruction. This again is in harmony with the very fundamental teaching of experience and is reasonable. So far from religion, then, being unreasonable, it is only the one lacking reason who rejects the revelation of life and immortality and says in his heart there is no God.

www.ingramcontent.com/pod-product-compliance
Lightning Source LLC
Chambersburg PA
CBHW032102230426
43672CB00009B/1615